The Victorious Attitude

Orison Swett Marden

The Victorious Attitude

Copyright © 2018 Bibliotech Press
All rights reserved

ISBN: 978-1-61895-340-7

TABLE OF CONTENTS

THE VICTORIOUS ATTITUDE

CHAPTER I

THE VICTORIOUS ATTITUDE

Go boldly; go serenely, go augustly;
Who can withstand thee then!
                                    Browning.

What a grasp the mind would have if we could always hold the victorious attitude toward everything! Sweeping past obstacles and reaching out into the energy of the universe it would gather to itself material for building a life in its own image.

To be a conqueror in appearance, in one's bearing, is the first step toward success. It inspires confidence in others as well as in oneself. Walk, talk and act as though you were a somebody, and you are more likely to become such. Move about among your fellowmen as though you believe you are a man of importance. Let victory speak from your face and express itself in your manner. Carry yourself like one who is conscious he has a splendid mission, a grand aim in life. Radiate a hopeful, expectant, cheerful atmosphere. In other words, be a good advertisement of the winner you are trying to be.

Doubts, fears, despondency, lack of confidence, will not only give you away in the estimation of others and brand you as a weakling, a probable failure, but they will react upon your mentality and destroy your self-confidence, your initiative, your efficiency. They are telltales, proclaiming to every one you meet that you are losing out in the game of life. A triumphant expression inspires trust, makes a favorable impression. A despondent, discouraged expression creates distrust, makes an unfavorable impression.

If you don't look cheerful and appear and act like a winner nobody will want you. Every man will turn a deaf ear to your plea for work. No matter if you are jobless and have been out of work for a long time you must keep up a winning appearance, a victorious

1

attitude, or you will lose the very thing you are after. The world has little use for whiners, or long-faced failures.

It is difficult to get very far away from people's estimate of us. A bad first impression often creates a prejudice that it is impossible afterwards wholly to remove. Hence the importance of always radiating a cheerful, uplifting atmosphere, an atmosphere that will be a commendation instead of a condemnation. Not that we should deceive by trying to appear what we are not, but we should always keep our best side out, not our second best or our worst. Our personal appearance is our show window where we insert what we have for sale, and we are judged by what we put there.

The victorious idea of life, not its failure side, its disappointed side; the triumphant, not the thwarted-ambition side, is the thing to keep ever uppermost in the mind, for it is this that will lead you to the light. You must give the impression that you are a success, or that you have qualities that will make you successful, that you are making good, or no recommendation or testimonial however strong will counteract the unfavorable impression you make.

So much of our progress in life depends upon our reputation, upon making a favorable impression upon others, that it is of the utmost importance to cultivate mental forcefulness. It is the mind that colors the personality, gives it its tone and character. If we cultivate will power, decision, positive instead of negative thinking, we cannot help making an impression of masterfulness, and everybody knows that this is the qualification that does things. It is masterfulness, force, that achieves results, and if we do not express it in our appearance people will not have confidence in our achieving ability. They may think that we can sell goods behind a counter, work under orders, carry out some mechanical routine with faithfulness and precision, but they will not think we are fitted for leadership, that we can command resources to meet possible crises or big emergencies.

Never say or do anything which will show the earmarks of a weakling, of a nobody, of a failure. Never permit yourself to assume a poverty-stricken attitude. Never show the world a gloomy, pessimistic face, which is an admission that life has been a disappointment to you instead of a glorious triumph. Never admit by your speech, your appearance, your gait, your manner, that there is anything wrong with you. Hold up your head. Walk erect. Look everybody in the face. No matter how poor you may be, or how shabby your clothes, whether you are jobless, homeless, friendless even, show the world that you respect yourself, that you believe in yourself, and that, no matter how hard the way, you are marching

2

on to victory. Show by your expression that you can think and plan for yourself, that you have a forceful mentality.

The victorious, triumphant attitude will put you in command of resources which a timid, self-depreciating, failure attitude will drive from you.

This was well illustrated by a visitor to the Athenæum Library in Boston. Ignorant of the fact that members only were entitled to its special privileges, this visitor entered the place with a confident bearing, seated herself in a comfortable window seat, and spent a delightful morning reading and writing letters. In the evening she called on a friend and in the course of conversation, referred to her morning at the Athenæum.

"Why, I didn't know you were a member!" exclaimed the friend.

"A member! No," said the lady. "I am not a member. But what difference does that make?"

The friend, who held an Athenæum card of membership, smiled and replied:

"Only this, that none but members are supposed to enjoy the privileges of which you availed yourself this morning!"

Our manner and our appearance are determined by our mental outlook. If we see only failure ahead we will act and look like failures. We have already failed. If we expect success, see it waiting for us a little bit up the road, we will act and look like successes. We have already succeeded. The failure attitude loses; the victorious attitude wins.

Had the lady in Boston had any doubt of her right to enter the Athenæum and freely to use all its conveniences, her manner would have betrayed it. The library attendants would have noticed it at once, and have asked her to show her card of membership. But her assured air gave the impression that she was a member. Her victorious attitude dominated the situation, and put her in command of resources which otherwise she could not have controlled.

The spirit in which you face your work, in which you grapple with a difficulty, the spirit in which you meet your problem, whether you approach it like a conqueror, with courage, a vigorous resolution, with firmness, or with timidity, doubt, fear, will determine whether your career will be one grand victory or a complete failure.

It is a great thing so to carry yourself wherever you go that when people see you coming they will say to themselves, "Here comes a winner! Here is a man who dominates everything he touches."

Thinking of yourself as habitually lucky will tend to make you so, just as thinking of yourself as habitually unlucky and always talking about your failures and your cruel fate will tend to make you unlucky. The attitude of mind which your thoughts and convictions produce is a real force which builds or tears down. The habit of always seeing yourself as a fortunate individual, the feeling grateful just for being alive, for being allowed to live on this beautiful earth and to have a chance to make good will put your mind in a creative, producing attitude.

We should all go through life as though we were sent here with a sublime mission to lift, to help, to boost, and not to depress and discourage, and so discredit the plan of the Creator. Our conduct should show that we are on this earth to play a magnificent part in life's drama, to make a splendid contribution to humanity.

The majority of people seem to take it for granted that life is a great gambling game in which the odds are heavily against them. This conviction colors their whole attitude, and is responsible for innumerable failures.

In the betting machines used by horse racing gamblers the bettors make the odds. If, for example, five hundred persons bet on a certain horse, and a hundred bet on another, then the first horse automatically becomes a five to one choice, and the odds in favor of his winning are five to one. In the game of life most of us start out by putting the odds on our failure.

In horse race gambling the judgment that forms the basis of belief as to the winning horse has a comparatively secure foundation in a knowledge of the qualifications of the different racers. In life gambling it is merely the unsupported opinion or viewpoint of the individual that puts the odds against himself. The majority of people look on the probability of their winning out in the life game in any distinctive way as highly improbable. When they look around and see how comparatively few of the multitudes of men and women in the world are winning they say to themselves, "Why should I think that I have a greater percentage of chance in my favor than others about me? These people have as much ability as I have, perhaps more, and if they can do no more than grub along from hand to mouth, of what use is it for me to struggle against fate?"

When people believe and figure that they cannot, and therefore never will, be successes, and conduct themselves according to their conviction: when they take their places in life not as probable winners, but as probable losers, is it any wonder that the odds are heavily against them?

"Mad! Insane! Eccentric!" we say when some miserable recluse dies in squalor and wretchedness,— "Starved," the coroner's inquest finds, although bank books revealing large deposits, or else hoards of gold, are discovered hidden away in nooks and crannies of the wretched miser's quarters.

Are such persons, whom we call mad, insane, eccentric, who stint and save, and hoard in the midst of plenty, refusing even to buy food to keep them alive, any worse than those who face life in a poverty-stricken, failure attitude, refusing to see and enjoy the riches, the glories all around them? Is it any wonder that life is a disappointment to them? Is it any wonder that they see only what they look for, get only what they expect?

What would you think of an actor who was trying to play the part of a great hero, but who insisted on assuming the attitude of a coward, and thinking like one; who wore the expression of a man who did not believe he could do the thing he had undertaken, who felt that he was out of place, that he never was made to play the part he was attempting? Naturally you would say the man never could succeed on the stage, and that if he ever hoped to win success, the first thing he should do would be to try to think himself the character, as well as to look the part, he was trying to portray. That is just what the great actor does. He flings himself with all his might into the rôle he is playing. He sees himself as, and feels that he is actually, the character he is impersonating. He lives the part he is playing on the stage, whether it be that of a beggar or a hero. If he is playing the part of a hero he acts like a hero, thinks and talks like a hero. His very manner radiates heroism. And vice versa, if the part he takes is that of a beggar, he dresses like one, thinks like one, bows, cringes and whines like a beggar.

Now, if you are trying to be successful you must act like a successful person, carry yourself like one, talk, act and think like a winner. You must radiate victory wherever you go. You must maintain your attitude by believing in the thing you are trying to do. If you persist in looking and acting like a failure or a very mediocre or doubtful success, if you keep telling everybody how unlucky you are, and that you do not believe you will win out because success is only for a few, that the great majority of people must be hewers of wood and drawers of water, you will be about as much of a success as the actor who attempts to personate a certain type of character while looking, thinking and acting exactly like its opposite.

By a psychological law we attract that which corresponds with our mental attitude, with our faith, our hopes, our expectations, or with our doubts and fears. If this were fully understood, and used as a working principle in life, we would have no poverty, no failures, no criminals, no down-and-outs. We would not see people everywhere with expressions which indicate that there is very little enjoyment in

5

living; that it is a serious question with them whether life is really worth while, whether it really pays to struggle on in a miserable world where rewards are so few and uncertain and pains and penalties so numerous and so certain.

Every boy, every girl should be taught to assume the victorious attitude toward life. All through a youth's education the idea should be drilled into him that he is intended to be a winner in life, that he is himself a prince, a god in the making. From his cradle up he should be taught to hold his head high, and to look on himself as a son of the King of kings, destined for great things.

No child is properly reared and educated until he or she knows how to lead a victorious life. This is what true education means— victory over self, victory over conditions.

It always pains me to hear a youth who ought to be full of hope and high promise express a doubt as to his future career. To hear him talk about his possible failure sounds like treason to his Creator. Why, youth itself is victory. Youth is a great prophecy, the forerunner of a superb fulfillment. A young man or a young woman talking about failure is like beauty talking about ugliness; like superb health dwelling upon weakness and disease; like perfection dwelling upon imperfection. Youth means victory, because everything in the life of the healthy boy or girl is looking upward. There is no downgrade in normal youth; it is its nature to climb, to look up. Its very atmosphere should breathe hope, superb promise of the future.

If all children were reared with such a triumphant conception of life, with such an unshakable belief in their heritage from God, that nothing could discourage them, we would hear no talk of failure; we would soon sight the millenium. If they were made to understand that there is only one failure to be feared,—failure to make good, the failure of character, the failure to keep growing, to ennoble and enrich one's life,—this world would be a paradise.

Just think what would happen if all of the down-and-outs to-day, all of the people who look upon themselves as failures or as dwarfs of what they ought to be, could only get this victorious, this triumphant, idea of life, if they could only once glimpse their own possibilities and assume the triumphant attitude! They would never again be satisfied to grovel. If they once got a glimpse of their divinity, once saw themselves in the sublime robes of their power, they never again would be satisfied with the rags of their poverty.

But instead of trying to improve their condition, to get away from their failure, poverty-stricken atmosphere, they cling the more closely to it and sink deeper and deeper in the quagmire of their own making. Everywhere we find whining, miserable people grumbling at everything, complaining that "life is not worth living," that "the game is not worth the candle," that "life is a cheat, a losing game."

Life is not a losing game. It is always victorious when properly played. It is the players who are at fault. The great trouble with all failures is that they were not started right. It was not drilled into the very texture of their being in youth that what they would get out of life must be created mentally first, and that inside the man, inside the woman, is where the great creative processes of life are carried on.

That which man does with his hands is secondary. It is what he does with his brain that counts. That is what starts things going. Some of us never learn how to create with our minds. We depend too much upon creating with our hands, or on other people to help us. We depend too much on the things outside of us when the mainspring of life, the power that moves the world of men and things, is inside of us.

There are times when we cannot see the way ahead, when we seem to be completely enveloped in the fogs of discouragement, disappointment and failure of our plans, but we can always do the thing that means salvation for us, that is persistently, determinedly, everlastingly to face towards our goal whether we can see it or not. This is our only chance of overcoming our difficulties. If we turn about face, turn our back on our goal, we are headed toward disaster.

No matter how many obstacles may block your path, or how dark the way, if you look up, think up, and struggle up, you can't help succeeding. Whatever you do for a living, whatever fortune or misfortune may come to you, hold the victorious attitude and push ahead.

A captain might as well turn about his ship when he strikes a fog bank, because he cannot see the way ahead of him, and still expect to make his distant harbor, as for you to drop your victorious attitude and face the other way just because you have run into a fog bank of disappointment or failure. The only hope of the captain's reaching his destination is in being true to the compass that guides him in the fog and darkness as well as in the light. He may not see the way, but he can follow his compass. That we also can do by holding the victorious attitude towards life, the only attitude that can insure safety and bring us into port.

CHAPTER II

"ACCORDING TO THY FAITH"

"Where there is Faith there is Love,
Where there is Love there is Peace,
Where there is Peace there is God,
Where there is God there is no need."

There is a divine voice within us which only speaks when every other voice is hushed,—only gives its message in the silence.

"I shall study law," said an ambitious youngster, "and those who are already in the profession must take their chances!"

The divine self-confidence of youth, the unshaken faith that believes all things possible, often makes cynics and world-weary people smile. Yet it is the grandest, most helpful attribute of man, the finest gift of the Creator to the race. If we could retain through life the faith of ambitious, self-confident, untried youth, its unquestioning belief in its ability to carve out its ideal in the actual, what wonders we should all accomplish! Such faith would enable us literally to remove mountains.

All through the Scriptures faith is emphasized as a tremendous power. It was by faith that Moses led the children of Israel out of Egypt, through the waters of the Red Sea, and through the wilderness. It was by faith that Elijah, Isaiah, Daniel, and all of the great prophets performed their miracles.

Faith was the great characteristic of Christ Himself. The word was constantly on His lips, "According to thy faith be it unto thee." He often referred to it as the measure of what we receive in life, also as the great healer, the great restorer. Whenever He healed He laid the entire emphasis upon the faith of the healer and the one healed. "Thy faith hath made thee whole," "Believe only and she shall be made whole," "Thy faith hath saved thee." Or He reproved His disciples for the lack of faith which prevented them from healing, as when He addresses them, "O faithless and perverse generation, how long shall I be with you and suffer you."

Faith believes; doubt fears. Faith creates; doubt destroys. Faith opens the door to all things desirable in life; doubt closes them. Faith is an arouser, an awakener of our creative forces. It opens the

8

door of ability and arouses creative energies. Faith is the link in the Great Within which connects man with his Maker. It is the divine messenger sent to guide men, blinded by doubt and sin. Our faith puts us in touch with Infinite Power, opens the way to unbounded possibilities, limitless resources. No one can rise higher than his faith. No one can do a greater thing than he believes he can. The fact that a person believes implicitly that he can do what may seem impossible to others, shows there is something within him that has gotten a glimpse of power sufficient to accomplish his purpose.

Men who have achieved great things could not account for their faith; they could not tell why they had an unflinching belief that they could do what they undertook. But the mere fact of such belief was evidence that they had had a glimpse of interior resourcefulness, reserve power and possibilities which would warrant that faith; and they have gone ahead with implicit confidence that they would come out all right, because this faith told them so. It told them so because it had been in communication with something that was divine, that which had passed the bounds of the limited and had veered into the limitless.

Men and women who have left their mark on the world have been implicit followers of their faith when they could see no light; but their unseen guide has led them through the wilderness of doubt and hardship into the promised land.

When we begin to exercise self-faith, self-confidence, we are stimulating and increasing the strength of the faculties which enable us to do the thing we have set our heart on doing. Our faith causes us to concentrate on our object, and thus develops power to accomplish it. Faith tells us that we may proceed safely, even when our mental faculties see no light or encouragement ahead. It is a divine leader which never misdirects us. But we must always be sure that it is faith, and not merely egotism or selfish desire that is urging us. There is a great difference between the two, and no one who is true to himself can possibly be deceived.

When we are doing right, when we are on the right track, our faith in the divine order of things never wavers. It sustains in situations which drive the self-centered egoist to despair. The man who does not see the Designer behind the design everywhere, who does not see the mighty Intelligence back of every created thing, cannot have that sublime faith which buoys up the great achievers and civilization-builders.

Our supreme aim should be to get the best from life, the best in the highest sense that life has to give, and this we cannot do without superb faith in the Infinite. What we accomplish will be large or small according to the measure of this faith. It is the man who

9

believes in the one Source of All who believes most in himself; it is the man who sees good in everything, who sees the divine in his fellow-man, who has faith in everybody, who is the master man. The skeptic, the pessimist, has no bulwark of faith, none of the divine enthusiasm that faith gives, none of the zeal that carries the man of faith unscathed through the most terrible trials.

Without confidence in the beneficence of the great universal plan we can not have much confidence in ourselves. To get the best out of ourselves we must believe that there is a current running heavenward, however much our surroundings may seem to contradict this. We must believe that the Creator will not be foiled in His plan, and that everything will work together for good, however much wars and crime, poverty, suffering and wretchedness all about us may seem to deny this.

The abiding faith in a Power which will bring things out right in the end, which will harmonize discord, has always been strong in men and women who have done great things in the world, especially in those who have achieved grand results in spite of the most severe trials and tribulations.

It takes sublime faith to enable a man to fight his way through "insuperable" difficulties, to bear up under discouragements, afflictions and seeming failure without losing heart; and it is just such faith that has characterized every great soul that has ever made good. Whatever other qualities they may have lacked, great characters have always had sublime faith. They have believed in human nature. They have believed in men. They have believed in the beneficent Intelligence running through the universe.

Some of the most important reforms in history have been brought about by very fragile, delicate men and women, not only without outside encouragement, but in the teeth of the most determined opposition. They have agitated and agitated, hoped and hoped, and struggled and struggled, until victory came. No one could even attempt the herculean tasks they accomplished without that instinctive, abiding faith in a Power superior to their own,—a Power which would work in harmony with honesty, with earnestness, with integrity of purpose, in a persistent struggle for the right, but which would never sanction wrong.

Think of what the faith of St. Paul enabled him to do for the world! Think of what Christ's little band of chosen disciples succeeded in accomplishing in spite of the might of the Roman empire pitted against them! The power of the greatest benefactors of the race came largely from the inspiration of faith in their mission, their belief that they were born to deliver a certain message to the world, that they were to make an important contribution to civilization. Think of what the faith of the inventor has done! It has kept him at his task, kept him nerved and encouraged in the face of starvation, kept him at his work when his family had gone back on him, when his neighbors had denounced him, and called him insane. Think of what the faith of Columbus, of Luther, of the Wesleys, has accomplished for mankind! It has ever been men with indomitable faith that have moved the world. They have been the great pioneers of progress.

An instinctive faith in the Divine Force which permeates the universe, which is friendly to the right and antagonistic to the wrong, has ever been the unseen helper that supported, encouraged, and stimulated men and women to accomplish the "impossible," or that which to lower natures seems beyond human capacity. It is this which sustains brave souls in adversity and enables them to bear up, to believe and hope and struggle on when everything seems to go against them. It is the same principle which supported the martyr at the stake and enabled him to smile when the flames were licking the flesh from his bones.

Faith has ever been the greatest power in civilization. It has built our railroads, has revealed the secrets of nature to science, has led the way to all our inventions and discoveries, and has brought success out of the most inhospitable conditions and iron environments. In fact, we owe everything that has been accomplished to faith, and yet when we come to its practical application in our everyday affairs how few of us avail ourselves of this tremendous force! The vast majority are looking for some power outside to help, when we ourselves hold the key which has ever unlocked, and ever will unlock, all barred doors to aspiring souls.

If people could only realize what a potent building, creative force faith is, and would exercise it in their daily lives, we should have very few paupers, very few failures, very few sickly, diseased or criminal among us. If, by some magic, a strong, vigorous faith could be injected into the men and women of the great failure army to-day, the larger part of them would get out of this army and get into the army of the successful.

It is not alone in our life work, or in great or special undertakings that faith is necessary. We need it every moment of our lives, in everything, great and small, that concerns us. It is just as necessary to your health as it is to your success. To build up the faith habit, faith in human nature, the habit of believing in yourself, in your ability, of believing that you are sane, sound, and level headed, that you have good judgment and good horse sense, that you are victory organized and that you are going to attain your ambition, is to blaze a path to success.

A man begins to deteriorate, to go toward failure, not when he loses all of his material possessions, not when he fails in his undertakings, but when he loses faith in himself, in his ability to make his dreams come true.

When we remember that self-faith characterizes successful people, and lack of it the mediocres and the failures, one would think that everybody would cultivate this divine quality which by itself alone has done so much for the individual and for the world.

The reason why faith works such marvels is that it is the leader of all the other mental faculties. They will not proceed until faith goes ahead. It is the basis of courage, of initiative, of enthusiasm. Much of Napoleon's power and early success came from his tremendous faith in his mission, the conviction that he was a man of destiny, that he was born under a lucky star, born to conquer. Shorn of his mighty belief in his star, stripped of the faith that he was born to rule, he would have been no more of a power in human affairs than the dullest private in the ranks of his army. When warned by his generals not to expose himself to the enemy, he would reply that the bullet or the cannon had not been cast which could kill Napoleon. This invincible belief in his destiny added wonderfully to his natural powers.

It was her conviction that she was chosen of God to free France from its enemies that made Joan of Arc, the simple, ignorant peasant girl of Domrèmy, the saviour of her country. Her mighty faith in her divine mission gave her a dignity and a miraculous force of character, a positive genius, that made all the commanders of the French army obey her as private soldiers obey their superior officers. Faith in herself and in her mission transformed the peasant maiden into the greatest military leader of her time.

There is no doubt that every human being comes to this earth with a mission. We are not accidental puppets thrown off to be buffeted by luck or chance or cruel fate. We are a part of the great universal plan. We were made to fit into this plan, to play a definite part in it. We come here with a message for humanity which no one else but ourselves can deliver, and faith in our mission, the belief that we are important factors in the great creative plan, that we are, in fact, co-creators with God, will add wonderfully to the dignity and effectiveness of our lives, will enable us to perform the "impossible."

If every child were brought up in the firm belief that he was made for health, happiness, and success; if it were impressed on him that he should never entertain a doubt of his power to attain them, as a man he would be infinitely stronger in his powers of self-assertion and in his self-confidence; and these qualities strengthen the ability, unify the faculties, clarify the vision, and make the attainment of what the heart yearns for a hundred per cent. more probable than if he had not been thus reared.

A child's faith is instinctive, and if not tampered with, destroyed by wrong training, would continue through life. We see this sort of instinctive faith illustrated by the lower animals. Take the birds, or the domestic hen, for example. See how patiently she sits on the eggs week after week until the chickens are hatched. She cannot see the chickens when she begins to sit, but her belief that they will come if she does her part induces her to give up her liberty for weeks, and to go sometimes for days without food, that she may keep the eggs at the right temperature in order to produce the chickens.

The trouble with most of us is that we do not have sufficient faith in the creative power of the vigorous determination to do a thing, in the persistent endeavor backed by self—faith to accomplish what we desire. We give up too easily under discouragement. We haven't sufficient stamina and grit to push on under disheartening conditions. We want to see clear through from the beginning to the end of whatever we undertake. We refuse to have faith. Yet much of the time throughout life we may have to work without any goal in sight, or at least without any clear light to see it, but if the mental attitude is right we know that, somehow, we shall attain our heart's desire. We have merely been shown a program which we are capable of carrying out, a table of contents of our capabilities, the signs of the corresponding realities, for faith is not an idle dream, an illusive picture of the imagination. We have not been mocked by ideals and aspirations, soul-yearnings and heart-longings for the things which have no possible realities. Faith is not a cheat. There is ability to match the faith.

There is something about devotion to one's inward vision, the intense desire and concentrated effort to fulfill what we believe to be our mission here, that has a solidifying influence upon the character, gives poise and peace of mind and also helps us to realize our vision.

The probabilities are that the iceberg which sent the Titanic, with sixteen hundred souls, to the bottom of the ocean did not even feel a tremor at the shock. More than seven-eighths of its huge bulk was below the water, deep down in the eternal calm of the sea, beyond the reach of storm or tempest. Like the giant iceberg, faith reaches down into the serene within of us, into the eternal calm of the soul. It is not disturbed by the surface commotions. A life poised in faith rides steadily, triumphantly, through the tempests and the hurricanes of existence.

You will constantly be confronted with things which tend to destroy faith in God and faith in yourself. There are many times in life when about all we can do is to hold on to the hand of the Divine Guide until we have run through the storm zone. We have to learn to turn away from the heart-breaks of life and to face toward the light. We have to disregard the criticisms and the discouragement of others, as well as the assaults of fear and doubt, and press on to our goal.

If you go in business for yourself, if you are struggling to get an education, if you are making desperate efforts to realize your ambition, whatever it is, you will find plenty of pessimists who will predict your failure. They will tell you that you never can build up a business without a lot of capital and outside help in these times of terrific competition, that you cannot work your way through college, that you can never be whatever you are dreaming of and longing to be. You will meet plenty of obstacles and much opposition, and it will take a very stiff backbone, a lot of sand and grit to keep pushing on towards your goal against great odds, but faith is more than a match for all these. Nothing else will enable you to win out.

Remember it is not other people's faith in you but your faith in yourself that counts most. It is a good thing to have other people's good opinion, to have their confidence in us, their faith in the success of our efforts, but it is not imperative. Our own is. No man ever gets anywhere or does anything great in this world without faith in himself, without a superb belief that he is on the right track, that he is doing the thing he was made to do, that he is going to stick to it through thick and thin to the end. It takes faith to look beyond obstacles, to see the way over difficulties, to brave opposition and to allow nothing to swerve us from our course.

You cannot keep any one from succeeding who has an unshakable faith in his mission. You cannot crush the faith that wrestles with difficulties, that never weakens under trials or afflictions, that pushes on when everybody else turns back, that gets up with greater determination every time it is knocked down.

In the sacred Confucian scriptures we are told that a very devoted disciple of Confucius, on a pilgrimage to his master, was stopped on his journey by a broad river. As he could not swim and could not procure a boat, the zealous disciple resolved that he would walk on the water. Believing that the necessity of seeing his master was most urgent, and being filled with zeal in the performance of his mission, he boldly made the attempt—and succeeded. The record of this miracle is supposed by followers of Confucius to be just as authentic as the Bible account of the walking of Christ on the water.

If, like this zealot, you have faith in your power to overcome difficulties, nothing can keep you from your goal. If, like Joan of Arc, you believe you are appointed by God to perform a certain work, it will help you wonderfully to make good. It will dignify your life and your efforts, and thus save you from a thousand temptations to waste your time in frivolous pursuits. It will put a higher value upon your importance to the world. To feel that you have a divine mission that no one else can perform, that you came here with a sacred message for mankind, and that it is up to you to deliver it will add a wonderful motive for effectiveness in your life work. The consciousness that you are keeping faith with your Creator and with yourself, that you are keeping faith with your fellowmen and earning their respect and love, that you are keeping faith with a splendid life purpose, with your holiest vision, gives a satisfaction which nothing else can afford.

Cling to your faith no matter what happens. It is your best friend. Like the magnetic needle on the ship's deck, which will find the north star, no matter how dense the fog, how dark the night, or how threatening the tempest, your faith, even though you cannot see, will find the way. It sees the open road, beyond the mountain of difficulties which shuts out the vision of the other faculties.

Some time ago, during one of our periodical business crises, some newspapers made merry over a statement of President Wilson that the condition of the United States, illustrated by the fact that eighty thousand freight cars were at the time side-tracked along the lines of one of our great railroads alone, could be changed by psychology. One of these papers sarcastically suggested that if we should take a dose of the psychology remedy and go to sleep somewhere in the misty, cloudy lands of theory, and dream that those eighty thousand empty freight cars were moving, we should see them move.

Now, in spite of newspaper skepticism, I believe that the psychology remedy if applied in every financial, business, or other crisis would prove absolutely effective. If all the people of this country would persistently hold a mental attitude of faith in our prosperity, which is the birthright of the inhabitants of this land of plenty; if they would have faith that our vast resources would enable us to carry on business, regardless of conditions in Europe or elsewhere, and if they would act in accordance with their faith, there would be no idle freight cars, no lack of work, no lack of money at any time.

It is the mental attitude of the people of the United States that causes financial panics and recurrent "hard times." And there is something dead wrong in a state of mind which produces periodical crises, intervals of nationwide stagnation in a land with resources great enough to make every one of its citizens rich, in a land where the State of Texas alone could give every one of them a better living than the majority get to-day.

Before we can make business conditions stable we must have faith in the stability of our limitless wealth, in the opulence of the earth over which the Creator has given us control. We have got to hold the prosperous vision, to see better times with the mental eye, not dimly in the future, but now, to have more faith in our Maker, in our nation, in ourselves individually.

Why, if we analyze the matter, we will see that our unparalleled national prosperity has been built up largely by psychology. Its foundations had their root in the faith of our forefathers, in their belief in our country's possibilities.

We all know that faith has preceded every achievement in the world's history. The activities of the whole country to-day are based upon psychology, upon the mental attitude, the faith, the hope, the expectation of its inhabitants.

"Without a vision the people perish," and when our vision, our faith, shrivels, when it is obscured or displaced by doubt, fear, anxiety, lack of confidence, all our activities suffer accordingly.

With abundant crops, with a lowering death rate and increasing longevity of our people, with constantly growing educational facilities, America ought to register every day of every year a high water point of prosperity. But when a large portion of the people lack faith in the future, when, from time to time, uncertainty is in the air, when everybody is doubting and fearing, waiting to see what is coming next, of course business will stagnate. It will follow the prevailing mental attitude, hesitate, waver, doubt, stand still like the idle freight cars.

We are just beginning to see that faith is as much a real force as is electricity. It is faith that removes mountains—mountains of difficulty, of opposition, of doubt, of distrust. It clears the track of all obstructions. It makes stepping stones of stumbling blocks. Faith is the most powerful, the most sublime of human attributes. Without it the bottom would drop out of civilization. It is the fundamental principle of life. Faith is the basis of health, of success, of happiness, of love itself. It believes in, hopes, trusts, clings to the loved one in spite of all faults and sins. It is faith that heals, that achieves, that hopes. The very feeling of harmony between ourselves and our God, that which gives assurance, a sense of protection and of safety which nothing else can give, is born of our faith in Him, in whom we live and move and have our being.

We must realize and appreciate more and more our divinity, the fact that we are made in the image of our Creator and that we must partake consciously of His qualities. Then we will have more faith in our powers. When we are conscious of having qualities like His we can rise above apparent limitations, above hereditary weakness. It is all preëminently a question of holding the right thought—the thought that builds, the thought that creates, that produces, the thought that we have within us unlimited possibilities, which can be realized. A sublime self-faith is absolutely indispensable to all great achievement.

Let no one shake your faith in yourself. That is what brings you into closest connection with God. It is your mainstay. There is no magic like faith; it elevates, refines and multiplies the power of every other faculty.

Whether we are starting out in life, or going downhill on the other side, facing the transition we call death, faith is our bracer, the trusty leader that will never fail to guide us to the home of our heart's desire.

If you are filled with a great faith you will not fear, though you walk through the valley of the shadow. Though the way may be dark faith will lead you into the light. The Power that has sustained you every moment of your existence, and without which you could not exist a fraction of a second, will certainly not leave you in your greatest need.

If you bade your child jump into your arms, he would not hesitate even though it was so dark that he could not see you. He would jump because of his faith in you. He would know that he would be perfectly safe in doing whatever you told him. Why should we fear to jump into the arms of the Infinite when we come to death's door, which is only the entrance to another life? Why should we fear to cross the valley that leads to the new life when we know that our great Father-Mother-God is on the other side waiting with outstretched arms to receive us?

> "I will not doubt; well anchored in the faith,
> Like some stanch ship, my soul braves every gale,
> So strong its courage that it will not fail
> To breast the mighty unknown sea of Death.
> Oh, may I cry when body parts with spirit,
> 'I do not doubt,' so listening worlds may hear it,
> With my last breath."

17

CHAPTER III

DOUBT THE TRAITOR

Faith is the torch that leads the way when the other faculties cannot see.
It is doubting and facing the wrong way, facing toward the black, depressing, hopeless outlook that kills effort and paralyzes ambition.
There is a divine current within us which would always flow Godward, always lead to our ultimate advantage, did we not obstruct it, or turn it aside by our doubts and fears.
He who has conquered doubt and fear has conquered failure.

James Allen.

When David Hume, the agnostic, was twitted with his inconsistency in going to hear the orthodox Scotch minister, John Brown, preach, he replied, "I don't believe all that he says, but he does, and once a week I like to hear a man who believes what he says."

If you utter a lie with the conviction that you are speaking the truth people will believe what you say, whereas if you proclaim a truth in a weak, hesitating voice, in a doubting manner, no one will believe you. If you should take a tray of genuine gold pieces upon the street and try to sell them, while showing by your very expression that you did not believe in what you had for sale, you could not dispose of those gold pieces for a tithe of their value. Nobody would believe either in their genuineness or in your own. Your timid, doubting, hesitating manner would queer all your chances of doing what you wanted to do.

I used to go trout fishing with two men, one of whom was always saying that he never had any luck fishing, that he somehow didn't have the knack, and never expected to catch many fish. This doubt totally unfitted him for successful trout fishing. He didn't take enough interest in the sport to study the habits and the haunts of the trout. He did not know the likely places in streams and rivers to drop his hook. He did not know the best kinds of bait to use. His doubt of his ability led to indifference, and this made him a failure as a trout fisher. The other man never had a doubt of success. If there were any trout to be caught he felt sure he would catch them.

18

For years he had made a study of trout habits. He could tell which side of the big rocks to cast his hook, and he knew how to cast it in a way that would tempt the trout. Fishing in the same stream alongside the doubtful, indifferent fisherman he would catch ten times as many fish.

If there is a great big doubt in your self-faith, if you have left a bridge standing for your retreat in case of defeat, if you lack clean-cut, firm decision, if there is any interrogation point in your confidence in yourself, there will be a limp in your success gait, and you will not be able to rise out of mediocrity.

Our worst enemies are not outside but inside of us. Every human being harbors a traitor who is always on the watch to thwart his ambition, to turn him aside from his aim. That traitor is doubt. You must make up your mind at the very outset of your career that you will always be followed about by certain mental enemies, mental traitors, which will try to dissuade you from doing the highest or biggest thing possible to you. Doubt is one of the most insistent of these, and will dog your steps to your grave. The man or woman who is not strong enough to resist its insidious attacks will never do what he or she is capable of doing, and was sent into the world by the Creator to do.

The person who is always fearful of consequences, who is in doubt as to the outcome of his acts, or whether he is really capable of doing what he undertakes, will always be a weakling. No one who is not bigger than his doubts can ever accomplish anything great or worth while, because this subtle enemy kills initiative and self-confidence, and without these dominant qualities no human being can measure up to his possibilities.

But for doubt, which strangles the very beginning of things, initiative instead of being so rare would be a common virtue among all classes. Nine out of ten average individuals are held back from testing their powers by the suggestions of doubt. If it were possible to drive from the human mind this specter which stands at the door of our hopes, of our resolution, which throws its baleful shadow across our vision, civilization would forge ahead by leaps and bounds. This miserable traitor, under the guise of a friend, is holding down millions of men and women below the level of their powers, keeping them from beginning things which they are capable of doing, but which doubt warns them at their peril not to attempt.

Doubt is responsible for more suicides, more misery, more bankrupt lives, more failures, than any other one thing. It makes more people afraid to start out on a course they know they ought to pursue than any other thing. Standing right at the gateway of our choice, at the parting of the ways, when we have fully resolved to take the path that is best for us, a hard and forbidding one compared with the easy way along the line of least resistance, doubt calls a halt. It bids us pause and think once more, asks us to look again at the rugged path we have chosen and consider whether we really want to pay the price of our choice, to take that turning when the other looks so much brighter and pleasanter and is so very much easier.

This is the point of cleavage which marks the beginning of failure for the timid soul who is not bigger than his doubt. The suggestions pushed into his mind by his enemy make him hesitate. He is moved to "stop, look, and listen." He begins to reconsider, to look again at the obstacles ahead, and the longer he looks the bigger they grow. He becomes frightened, fears he cannot do the thing that at first seemed possible, and finally turns aside to the easier path of mediocrity and commonness.

Doubt has killed more splendid projects, shattered more ambitious schemes, strangled more effective genius, neutralized more superb effort, blasted more fine intellects, thwarted more splendid ambitions than any other enemy of the race.

Talk about drug victims and slaves of drink! Doubt has more victims than even these terrible enemies of the race. We see them everywhere in menial and lowly positions, perpetual clerks, discontented drudges, hewers of wood and drawers of water, paralyzed at the very gateway of their career by that fatal trait which they have never learned how to strangle, to neutralize with its opposites, faith, hope, confidence, assurance.

How many thousands of employees plodding along in mediocrity to-day could have been in business for themselves but for this great enemy inside of them! How many splendid young men have been kept out of the pulpit, how many superb lawyers, in possibility, have been strangled by this traitor! How many men are to-day clerks, bookkeepers, or other subordinates, who might have been managers, superintendents or proprietors themselves but for the work of this damnable traitor!

When opportunity presented itself these doubters were afraid. They waited for certainty. They dared not take chances. They did not realize that opportunity is a maiden who admires the bold, courageous, self-confident suitor. They did not wake up in time to the fact that she will not trust herself to the timid, the hesitant, the over-cautious suitor. When too late they realized that while the doubter is wavering and hesitating, wondering if he dare try to win, the daring, intrepid wooer steps in and wins.

The great prizes of life are for the courageous, the dauntless, the self-confident. The timid, hesitating, vacillating man who listens to his doubts and fears stops to make up his mind, and—the opportunity has passed beyond his reach.

Doubt, uncertainty, or fear as to results, is the great discourager of the human race. It is the dire enemy of all achievement. It tells the poor boy and girl who long for an education that it is foolish for them to think of going through school and college without money or without somebody to help them. It tells them that there are many more poor boys and girls in every school and college who are trying to pay their way than will ever find opportunities to make their education available. It is always whispering to them that there is a big waiting list of men and women who were graduated years ago everywhere looking and waiting, trying in vain to get something to do to earn back the amount they spent on their education.

No matter what you attempt to do, what new enterprise you may undertake, what progressive plans you may make, the traitor doubt will bob up and call a halt, will try to dissuade you from your purpose. It will suggest to you how many others have undertaken similar things and have gone to the wall, have failed to accomplish what they expected. It will tell you that you had better go slow, that it is foolish to go into business in times like these, that you should wait until you are better prepared, until you have more capital; in short, that there are stumbling blocks in the way, and that you must consider the step very carefully before you venture to decide.

It does not matter what we plan to do, doubt is always there ready to knock our resolutions, and, if possible, to discourage us even from attempting to put our plans in execution. Who could ever estimate how many superb inventions and discoveries, which would have helped emancipate the race from drudgery and hard conditions, have been side-tracked by this traitor!

Doubt kills activity, discourages ambition and destroys or neutralizes the biggest brain power. It would make a pigmy of a Webster. By filling his mind full of doubt of his own creative power, a hypnotist could make a Shakespeare believe he was a fool. He could inject a doubt into the mind of a Napoleon that would cut his genius down to the mediocrity of a common soldier.

This arch traitor of mankind is so closely related to fear that it is almost impossible to draw a dividing line between the two. They are twins. Wherever doubt can get a foothold it introduces its brother fear, and fear brings with it all of its relatives, worry, anxiety, discouragement—the whole failure family. A single day of doubts, of fears, of unbeliefs, of the crime of self-depreciation, will drive away from a man all that he has attracted to himself in many months.

There are multitudes of people to-day suffering from the fatal disease of self-depreciation, the seeds of which were implanted in them by doubt. All the victims of discouragement, those who are suffering from despondency, those who are going through life disheartened, hopeless, despairing, are the authors of their own misery. They persist in killing the very thing they are pursuing, in queering their own quest by the poison of doubt.

The doubting Thomases never get anywhere, because they have no vision, and "without a vision the people perish." The man who would do anything worth while in this world must have a vision, and he must have courage to match it. Courage is the great leader in the mental realm. Whatever paralyzes it strangles the initiative, kills the ability to do things. Doubt is its greatest enemy. It suggests caution at the very moment when everything depends on boldness. If a general were to be over-cautious, to wait for absolute certainty in regard to results before putting his plan of campaign into action, he would never win a battle.

Caution is an admirable trait, but when carried to excess it ceases to be a virtue and comes perilously near being a vice. It may render ineffective many noble qualities. There are a great many people who seem to be courageous enough, but an excessive development of caution holds everything in abeyance to wait for certainty. I know men who wait and wait, never daring to undertake anything where there is risk, even though their judgment tells them they ought to go ahead.

We are creatures of habit, and the constant raising of doubts in our minds as to our ability to do what we want to do in time becomes a habit of thinking we can't, and when we think we can't, we can't. When a man begins to listen to his doubts he is beginning to weaken.

Why delay beginning the thing that you know perfectly well you ought to do? What are you afraid of? Failure, even, in an honorable attempt, is preferable to forever postponing the thing that you ought to do. Is it the additional responsibility you shrink from, the extra work? Do you have a horror of possible failure? Do you shrink from the possible humiliation of losing out in your venture? What is it that enlarges your doubt and holds you back? Some handicap, some invisible thread? Are you carrying a great excess of baggage, clinging to unnecessary things which handicap you?

I have heard of a sailor who lost his life in that way. He was one of the crew of a ship that was carrying a large quantity of gold nuggets to a distant port. The ship ran upon a rock, and, when all hope of saving her or her precious cargo was gone, the captain ordered everybody to leave the sinking ship. The last boat was ready to push off, but this sailor refused to get into it until he had loaded himself with gold nuggets. He said he had been a poor man all his life, and now he was going to be rich at last. He would take away with him just as much of the sinking wealth as he could carry. Heedless of the warning of the captain and his companions that they would not wait for him, he loaded himself with gold. Then, the boats having pushed away, he jumped overboard and tried to save himself by clinging to pieces of the wreck. But, owing to the weight he carried, he could neither float nor swim, and so the wealth he felt he could not leave behind carried him down to death.

Your doubt of your success is probably your biggest handicap. But it would be a thousand times better to make mistakes by forging ahead too rapidly, by undertaking more than we can carry out, than to be forever hovering upon the edge of doubt, delaying, postponing, waiting for certainty, until we become slaves of a habit which we cannot break. And remember that the habit of putting off, of waiting to see how things are going to turn out, to see if something more certain, something with less of risk, will not turn up, is fatal to initiative, fatal to leadership, fatal to efficiency.

I know a man who has been resolving for a quarter of a century to start something in which he thoroughly believes. Every year during that long period he has told me that this was the year for him to start. He was really going to begin his great life work, but doubt has engendered the putting off habit, and this has such a grip upon him that he shrinks from undertaking anything new. He seems to have a great fear of getting out of his old rut, to try something different, a fear that things may not work out right, that it is not the psychological moment to strike. He has gray hairs now, the enthusiasm of youth is gone, and he never will begin to do the thing which everybody who knows him believes he is perfectly capable of doing.

All history shows that while experience increases wisdom, it does not always increase faith. The inexperienced youth will often undertake things which stagger the older and more experienced. Confidence is characteristic of youth; but after a few setbacks and disappointments, many begin to wonder whether, after all, their first confidence was based upon good judgment, whether their enthusiasm and faith were not the result of lack of experience, and then they begin to doubt and to fear that this voice of ambition which is ever beckoning them on and upward is not reliable. They say to themselves: "What if this should be merely a mirage to lure me on the rocks," and before they realize it they are weaving doubts and fears and over-caution into a habit that has ruined multitudes of careers, a habit that is responsible for a larger percentage of unused ability, of locked-up powers than any other one thing.

Have you done the biggest thing you are capable of doing? Is it not possible that there is something within you, some unworked mental territory which, if cultivated, would lead you out into that wider field you dreamed of when a youth? Why do you go on year after year in the same old rut, expressing nothing, doing the same old thing in the same old way because doubt whispers it would be rash to try new ways, new ideas? How long have you been just an ordinary employee? Do you realize that habit is getting a tremendous grip upon you, and that before you realize it you may be a "perpetual clerk"?

The longer you remain in one position, doing the same thing without promotion, the stronger the inertia habit will grip you, the bigger will grow your doubt as to the wisdom of making a change. It is a dangerous thing to get into a rut. Bestir yourself before it is too late and begin to put into operation that plan which has so long haunted you, but which doubt has been telling you is not feasible, is not practicable.

If every human being to-day were doing what he has at least some time thoroughly believed he could do our whole civilization would be revolutionized. What has been accomplished is but a tithe of what might have been accomplished if every one had been true to his vision, had not allowed it to be blotted out by doubt. If I believed in a real devil I think it would be that unseen monitor, that mysterious something within us which whispers doubt, which tells us to hold on, to be careful, to go slow; which pulls us back when we are attempting to reach out, trying to do the thing we long to do.

Are you not tired of having your plans thwarted, your efforts blighted by the traitor, doubt? Has it not dwarfed your life long enough, has it not kept you out of your own long enough by forcing you to live on the husks when you might have had the kernel? Are you not about tired of being defrauded by this thief of the blessings and the good things which the Creator intended we all should have? Why not turn it out of your mental house? Neutralize it with a great splendid faith in yourself, in your mission, faith in your possible contribution to the world. Doubt has very little influence with the Saint Paul type of man, with the masterful type. It is only the weakling that doubt strangles, paralyzes. Be a man and not a weakling, a mere apology of a man.

You know that the devil which has followed you through life, which has blocked your progress, put out the lights in your path, tortured you and undermined your confidence in yourself, has been the devil of doubt. It has been the whispering fiend which told you that you could not do this and you could not do that, which stepped in and killed your initiative when you were about to begin to do that which your ambition had hoped to accomplish.

Don't let this enemy thwart and baffle you any longer. Have a good heart to heart talk with yourself and break the habit chain of unbelief in self with which it has bound you. Say to yourself, "I will not listen any longer to the voice of this fiend. I will not allow it to spoil God's plan for me. There is something inside of me which insists that I was planned for victory, not for defeat, for happiness, not for misery, for peace of mind, not for a life of worry, anxiety, and fear. I do not believe that I was placed here to be a mere puppet of circumstances. Faith, hope and confidence are my helpers. Doubt is a child of fear, and fear has the great majority of human beings hypnotized, so that they do not dare to forge ahead, do not dare to undertake the things they are perfectly capable of accomplishing. From henceforth it has no power over me. I will not listen to its treacherous voice."

If you would succeed, you must avoid rashness as well as over-caution. But when you have fully considered in all its bearings whatever project you are about to undertake, and have decided on your course, don't let any fears or doubts enter your mind. Commit yourself to your undertaking, and don't look back to see if you could have done something else, or started in some other way. Push on, and don't be afraid.

After we have launched out in an enterprise, have committed ourselves before the world, pride steps into the situation and pushes us on through hardships which would have discouraged and turned us aside before we had fully committed ourselves. But when we have taken the plunge, made the venture, we have practically said to the world, "Now, watch me make good. I have made up my mind to put this thing through, and I am not going to turn back." Our confidence grows as we advance and then it is comparatively easy, even under difficulties, to keep forging ahead.

Every child, every youth should be taught the danger of this fatal human enemy, doubt. They should be so imbued with the philosophy of expecting success instead of failure that doubt would never get sufficient grip on them to strangle their capabilities and blight the fulfillment of their dreams. If every child were reared with the conviction that he was born for happiness, that it was intended he should realize his vision, his mind would be turned towards the light, his whole mentality would be so firmly set toward success and happiness that doubt could not get hold of him. As it is the lives of multitudes of people are constantly filled with doubts and fears and uncertainty in regard to the future. Young impressionable minds are often stamped with the failure suggestion before they are out of their teens. Most of us are born with the doubt germ implanted in our brain.

There are hundreds of thousands of people in this country to-day who have splendid ambitions, who have made resolutions to carry out those ambitions, but who are cowering victims of doubt, which keeps them from making a start. They are just waiting. They are unable to make a beginning while this monster stands at the door of their resolution. They are afraid to burn their bridges behind them, to commit themselves to their purpose.

At the very outset of your career make up your mind that you are going to be a conqueror in life, that you are going to be the king of your mental realm, and not a slave to any treacherous enemy, that you will choose the wisest course, no matter how forbidding or formidable the difficulties in the way, that you will take the turning which points toward the goal of your ambition, no matter who or what may bar your onward path. Don't let doubt balk your efforts. Don't let it paralyze your beginning and make you a pigmy so that you will not half try to make good when you have a waiting giant in you. Confidence, self-assurance, self-faith—these are the great friends which will kill the traitor doubt.

CHAPTER IV

MAKING DREAMS COME TRUE

"Every great soul of man has had its vision and pondered it, until the passion to make the dream come true has dominated his life."

> *"You will be what you will to be;*
> *Let failure find its false content*
> *In that poor world 'environment,'*
> *But spirit scorns it, and is free.*
>
> *"The human Will, that force unseen,*
> *The offspring of a deathless Soul,*
> *Can hew a way to any goal,*
> *Though walls of granite intervene."*

Washington, in a letter written when he was but twelve years old, said: "I shall marry a beautiful woman; I shall be one of the wealthiest men in the land; I shall lead the army of my colony; I shall rule the nation which I help to create."

General Grant, in his "Memoirs," says that as a boy at West Point, he saw General Scott seated on his horse, reviewing the cadets, and something within him said, "Ulysses, some day you will ride in his place and be general of the army."

Every one knows how those boyish visions were realized by the mature men.

The late J. Pierpont Morgan's fortune was built largely by the dynamic forcefulness of his thought, of his mental visualizing, the nursing of his youthful visions. He was a man of varied and æsthetic tastes, but he concentrated upon finance and he became the world's master in its science.

Ancient Greece concentrated on beauty and art, and she became the great beauty model and art teacher of the world. The Roman Empire concentrated upon power—and became mistress of the world. England concentrated on the control of the seas and commerce, and she has become the ruler of the seas and the greatest commercial nation in the world. We are a nation of money-makers because Americans have concentrated largely upon the dollar. They think in its terms; they dream dollars; they hate poverty and they long for wealth.

27

Whatever an individual or a people concentrates upon it tends to get, because concentration is just as much of a force as is electricity. The youth who concentrates upon law, thinks law, dreams law, reads everything he can get hold of relating to law, steals into courts, listens to trials at every chance he gets, is sure to become a lawyer.

It is the same with any other vocation or art,—medicine, engineering, literature, music; any of the arts or sciences. Those who concentrate upon an idea, who continue to visualize their dreams, to nurse them, who never lose sight of their goal, no matter how dark or forbidding the way, get what they concentrate on. They make their minds powerful magnets to attract the thing on which they have concentrated. Sooner or later they realize their dreams.

What could have kept Ole Bull from becoming a master musician? Who or what could keep back a boy who would brave his father's displeasure, steal out of his bed at night, and go into the attic to play his "little red violin," which haunted his dreams and would not let him sleep? What could keep a Faraday or an Edison, whom no hardships frightened, from realizing the wonderful visions of boyhood?

If you can concentrate your thought and hold it persistently, work with it along the line of your greatest ambition, nothing can keep you from its realization. But spasmodic concentration, spasmodic enthusiasm, however intense, will peter out. Dreaming without effort will only waste your power. It is holding your vision, together with persistent, concentrated endeavor on the material plane, that wins.

There are thousands of devices in the patent office in Washington which have never been of any use to the world, simply because the inventors did not cling to their vision long enough to materialize it in perfection. They became discouraged. They ceased their efforts. They let their visions fade, and so became demagnetized and lost the power to realize them. Other inventors have taken up many such "near" successes, added the missing links in their completion and have made them real successes.

"Get thy spindle and distaff ready, and God will send the flax," saith the proverb. If we would only take God's promises to heart, and do our necessary part for their fulfillment no one would be unsuccessful or unhappy. If we were to send out our desires intensely; to visualize them until our very mentalities vibrated with the things we long for, and to work persistently in their direction, we would attract them.

Everywhere there are disappointed men and women who have

soured on life because they could not get what they longed for,—a musical or art education, the necessary training for authorship, for law or medicine, for engineering, or for some other vocation to which they felt they had been called. They are struggling along in an uncongenial environment, railing at the fate which has robbed them of their own. They feel that life has cheated them, when the truth is they have cheated themselves. They never got the spindle and distaff ready that would have drawn to them the flax for the spinning of a happy and complete life web. They did not insistently and persistently send out their desires and longings; they did not nurse them and positively refuse to give them up; above all, they did not put forth their best efforts for their realization.

Three things we must do to make our dreams come true. Visualize our desire. Concentrate on our vision. Work to bring it into the actual. The implements necessary for this are inside of us, not outside. No matter what the accidents of birth or fortune, there is only one force by which we can fashion our life material—mind.

The bee and the snake draw material from the same plant. The one transmutes it into deadly poison; the other into delicious honey. The power that changes the stuff into a new substance is within the bee and the snake.

Of two boys or two girls in the same wretched environment, one picks up an education, trains himself or herself for place and power, while the other grows up a nobody. It is all in the boy or the girl. Each has similar material to work in. One transmutes it into gold; the other into lead.

Two sailors force the same breeze to send their boats in opposite directions. It is not the wind, but the set of the sail that determines the port.

The power that makes our desire, our vision, a reality is not in our environment or in any condition outside of us; it is within us.

There is some unseen, unknown, magnetic force developed by a long-continued concentration of the mind upon a cherished desire that draws to itself the reality which matches the desire. We cannot tell just what this force is that brings the thing we long for out of the cosmic ether and objectifies it, shapes it to correspond with our longing. We only know that it exists. The cosmic ether everywhere surrounding us is full of undreamed of potencies and the strong, concentrated mind reaches out into this ether, this sea of intelligence, attracts to it its own, and objectifies the desire.

All human achievements have been pulled out of the unseen by the brain, through the mind reaching out and fashioning the wealth of material at its disposal into the shapes which matched the wishes, the desires, of the achievers.

29

All the great discoveries, great inventions, great deeds that have lifted man up from his animal existence have been wrought out of the actual by the perpetual thinking of and visualizing these things by their authors. These grand characters clung to their vision, nursed it until they became mighty magnets that attracted out of the universal intelligence the realization of their dreams.

Most revolutionary inventions have evolved from a flash of thought. The sewing machine, for example, started with a simple idea, which the inventor held persistently in his mind until through his efforts the idea materialized into the concrete reality. Elias Howe used to watch his wife making garments, sewing, sewing far into the night, and it set him thinking, questioning whether such drudgery was really necessary. As he watched her busy needle fly back and forth, he began to wonder if this same work which it took his wife so long to do could not be done with less labor and in half the time by some sort of mechanical contrivance. He kept nursing his idea, thinking what a splendid thing it would be if some one could relieve millions of women from this toil, which frequently had to be done at night after a day of hard work. He began to experiment with crude devices, clinging to his vision through poverty and the denunciation of friends, who thought the man must be crazy to spend his time on "such a fool idea." But at last his vision materialized into a marvelous reality, a perfected machine which has emancipated the women of the world from infinite drudgery.

The idea of the telephone was flashed into the mind of Professor Alexander Bell by the drawing of a string through a hole in the bottom of a tin can, by means of which he found that the voice could be transmitted. The idea took such complete possession of the inventor that it robbed him of sleep and, for a time, made him poor. But nothing could rob him of his vision or prevent him from struggling to work it out of the visionary stage into the actual.

I lived near Professor Bell, in the next room, indeed, while he worked on his invention. I saw much of his struggle with poverty, heard the criticisms and denunciations of his friends, as he persisted in his visionary work until the telephone became a reality,—a reality without which modern business could not be conducted.

All of Edison's inventions, those of every inventor, have been wrought out on the same principle that gave us the sewing machine and the telephone. They all started in simple ideas, in dream visions which were nursed and worked into actualities.

According to Darwin, the desire to ascend into the heavens preceded the appearance and development of the eagle's wings. It is

30

said our different organs and functions have been developed from a sense of need of them, just as the wings of the eagle developed from a desire to fly.

The brain cells grow in response to desire. Where there is no desire there is no growth. The brain develops most in the direction of the leading ambition, where the mental activities are the most pronounced. The desire for a musical career, for instance, develops the musical brain cells. Business ambition develops that part of the brain which has to do with business, the cells which are brought into action in executive management, in administering affairs, in money making. Wherever we make our demand upon the brain by desire that part responds in growth.

For years a poor country boy builds air castles of his future. He visualizes the great mercantile establishment over which he is to preside. The ridicule of his family and of young companions cannot daunt him or blur the bright vision he sees away in the distance. He continues to nurse his vision, and behold, out of the unknown, unexpected resources come, and soon he finds himself an office boy in a great mercantile house in the city of his dreams. He watches everything with an eagle eye; he absorbs information and ideas; he is alert, active, energetic, resourceful, and in a few months he is promoted, and then again promoted. He attracts the attention of the head of the establishment, who calls him into his private office, tells him that he has had his eye on him for many months and that he believes he is the youth he has been looking for to manage the business. He gives him a little stock; the business prospers still further under his management, and in a few years the new manager is made a full partner in the house which he entered as an office boy. This is the flowering out of his dream, the objectifying of his vision, the matching with reality his youthful longings. His brain has been continually developing along the line of his vision, drawing to him the material to make it real.

A poor girl, the daughter of humble people in Maine who thought that to become a public singer was an unforgivable sin, could not in the beginning see any possible way to realize the dreams she held in secret, but she kept visualizing her dream, nursing her desire and doing the only thing for its realization her parents would allow,— singing in a little church choir. Gradually the way opened, and one step led to another until the little Maine girl became the famous Madame Nordica, one of the world's greatest singers.

No matter if you are a poor girl away back in the country, and see no possible way of leaving your poor old father and mother in order to prepare for your career, don't let go of your desire. Whether it be music, art, literature, business or a profession, hold to it. No matter how dark the outlook, keep on visualizing your desire and light and opportunity will come to enable you to make it a reality. Whatever the Creator has fitted you to do He will give you a chance to do, if you cling to your vision and struggle as best you can for its attainment.

Think of the Lillian Nordicas, the Lucy Stones, the Louisa Alcotts, the Mary Lyons, the Dr. Anna Howard Shaws, the thousands of women who were hedged in just as you are, by poverty or forbidding circumstances of some sort, yet succeeded in spite of everything in doing what they desired to do, in being what they longed to be. Take heart and believe that God has given you also "all implements divine to shape the way" to your soul's desire.

If you are a boy on a farm and feel that you are a born engineer, yet see no possible way to get a technical education, don't lose heart or hope. Get what books you can on your specialty. Cling to your vision. Push out in every direction that is possible to you. It may take years, but if you are true to yourself your concentration on your desire, your pushing toward it, will open a door into the light, and before you know it you will be on the road to your goal.

The Washingtons, the Lincolns, the Faradays, the Edisons, the men who have done most for their country and for humanity have had to struggle as hard as you are struggling to attain their heart's desire. The opportunities for boys and girls to bring out whatever the Creator has implanted in them are ten to one to-day to what they were one hundred, or fifty, or even twenty-five years ago. The great danger in our time is not lack of chance or opportunity but of losing our vision, of letting our ambition die.

Most of us instead of treating our desires seriously trifle with them as though they were only to be played with, as though they never could be realities. We do not believe in their divinity. We regard our heart longings, our soul yearnings as fanciful vagaries, romances of the imagination. Yet we know that every invention, every discovery or achievement that has blessed the world began in a desire, in a longing to produce or to do a certain thing, and that the persistent longing was accompanied by a struggle to make the mental picture a reality.

It is difficult for us to grasp the fact that ambition, accompanied by effort, is actually a creative power which tends to realize itself. Our minds are like that of the doubting disciple, who would not believe that his Lord had risen until he had actually thrust his finger into the side which had been pierced by a cruel spear. Only the things that we see seem real to us when, as a matter of fact, the most real things in the world are the unseen.

We never doubt the existence of the force that brings the bud out of the seed, the foliage and the flower out of the bud, the fruits, the vegetables from the flower. It is invisible. We cannot sense it, but we know that it is mightier than anything we see. No one can see or hear or feel gravitation, or the forces which balance the earth and whirl it with lightning speed through space, bringing it round its orbit without a variation of the tenth of a second in a century, yet who can doubt their reality? Does any one question the mighty power of electricity because it cannot be seen or heard or smelled?

The potency of our desires, of our soul longings, when backed by the effort to make them realities, is just as real as is that of any of the unseen forces in Nature's great laboratory. The great cosmic ether is packed with invisible potentialities. Whatever comes out of it to you comes in response to your call. Everything you have accomplished in life has been a result of a psychic law which, consciously or unconsciously, you have obeyed.

Do not make the mistake of thinking that the way will not open because you cannot now see any possible means of achieving that for which you long. The very intensity of your longing for a certain career, to do a certain thing, is the best evidence that you have the ability to match it, and that this ability was given you for a purpose, even to play a divine, a magnificent part in the great universal plan. The longing is merely the forerunner of achievement. It is the seed that will germinate if nurtured by effort.

If, however, you stop at sowing the seed you will get just about as much harvest as a farmer would get if he should sow his seeds without preparing the soil, without fertilizing or cultivating it or keeping down the weeds. It is the blending of the practical with the ideal that brings the harvest from the seed thought. You must keep on struggling toward your ideal. No matter how black and forbidding the way ahead of you, just imagine you are carrying a lantern which will advance with you and give light enough for the next step. It is not necessary to see to the end of the road. All the light you need is for the next step. Faith in your vision and persistent endeavor will do the rest. There is no doubt that if we do our part, the Divinity that has created us, given us an appointed place and a work in the plan of the universe, will bring things out better than we can plan or even imagine.

Send out your wishes, cherish your desires, force out your yearnings, your heart longings with all the intensity and persistency you can muster, and you will be surprised to see how soon they will begin to attract their affinities, how they will grow and take tangible shape, and ultimately become actual things. Fling out your desires

33

into the cosmic ether boldly, with the utmost confidence. Therein you will gather the material which shall build into reality the castle of your dreams.

The trouble with us is that we are afraid to do this. We fear that fate will mock us, cast back to us our mental visions empty of fruition. We do not understand the laws governing our thought forces any more than we understand the laws governing the universe. If we had faith in their power, our earnest thoughts and efforts would germinate and bud and flower just as does the tiny seed we put into the earth.

Think how the seed must be tended and nurtured before it will give forth the new life. See how the delicate bud has to be coaxed by the sun and air for many months before it pushes its head up through the tough sod to the light. Suppose it were afraid to make the attempt and should say: "It is impossible for me to get out of this dark earth. There is no light here. I am so tender the slightest pressure will break me and stop my growth forever. The only way out of my prison is to push up through this tough sod, and it would take a tremendous force to do that. I would be crushed, strangled, before I got half way through."

But the sun beckons, coaxes, encourages. The bud is moved into attempting the "impossible," and behold, in a few days it rears its tender head above what it considered the great enemy of its progress. The dark sod, the very thing which it thought was going to make its future impossible, becomes its support and strength. The very struggle to get up through the soil has strengthened its fiber and fitted it to cope with the elements above, with the storms it must meet.

Just like this tender plant, you may be hemmed in by seemingly insurmountable obstacles; you may not see a ray of light through the sod of hard, forbidding circumstances, but hold your vision and keep pushing. In your struggle you will develop strength, you will find sunshine and air, growth and life. You may be shut in by an uncongenial occupation and tempted to lose heart and give up your dreams because you can see no way to better yourself. This is just the time to cling to them, and to insist that they shall come true. Without knowing it you may be just in the middle of the sod, and if you keep pushing where you are, in season and out of season, you will come to the sunlight and the air, to freedom.

There is no human being who doesn't have some sort of a chance. If your present position cramps you; if it does not give you room to express yourself, you can make room by filling it to overflowing, by doing your work as well as it can be done, by keeping your mind steadfastly fixed on the ladder of your ascent. In your mind you make the stairs by which you ascend or descend. Nobody else can do it for you. The master key which will unlock that cruel door that keeps you back is not in the hand of fate. You are fashioning it by your thoughts.

Your next step is right where you are, in the thing you are doing to-day. The door to something better is always in the duty of the moment. The spirit in which you do your work, the energy which you throw into it, the determination with which you back up your ambition—these, no matter what opposes, are the forces that unlock the door to something better. If you hold to your vision and are honest, earnest and true, there is nothing that can stand in the way of its realization.

I have never known a person who was dead-in-earnest in his efforts to gain his heart's desire who has not finally reached his goal. No great, insistent, persistent, honest longing backed by downright hard, conscientious work ever comes back empty-handed.

Desire is at the bottom of every achievement. We are the product of our desires. What we long for, strive for, the vision we nurse, is our great life shaper, our character molder.

Very few can realize the close coördination which exists between their visions, their mind pictures, and the actual accomplishments of their career. If I were asked to name the principal cause of the majority of failures in life I should say it was the failure to understand this, to grasp the relation of thought to accomplishment. The gradual fading out of one's dreams, the losing of one's vision, may be traced to this cause.

When we first start out in life we are enthusiasts. Our vision is bright and alluring, and we feel confident we are going to win out, that we shall do something distinctive, something individual, unusual. But after a few setbacks and failures we lose heart, and faith in our vision dies. Then we gradually awaken to the fact that our ambition is beginning to deteriorate. It is not quite as sharply defined as formerly. Our ideals are a trifle dimmed, our longings a trifle less insistent. We try to find reasons and excuses for our lagging efforts and waning enthusiasm. We think it may be due to over-work; because we are tired and need a rest, or because our health is not quite up to standard, and that by and by our former intense desire to realize our dreams will return. But the whole process is so insidious that before we realize it our fires, for lack of fuel, are quite burned out. Our grip on our vision was not strong enough. We did not half understand its mighty power, when firmly and persistently kept in mind, to help us to our goal.

35

What we get out of life depends very largely on fidelity to our visions. If we believe in them we will not let them die for lack of nursing. If we really have ability to match them, and are not self-deceived by egotism, petty vanity and conceit, no misfortunes, no failure of plans, no discouragements, no obstacles, nothing in the world can separate us from them. We will cling to them to our dying day.

The man who believes in his life vision, who is not a mere egotist or idle dreamer, who sees in his desire a prophecy of something which he is perfectly able to make come true,—he is the man who has ever made the world move. He flings his life into his effort to match his vision with its reality.

The world stands aside for such a one, for one who believes in his vision, who consecrates himself without reserve to its fulfillment. People know there is something back of the dreamer who has such faith in his life dream that he will sacrifice everything to make it come true.

How much of a grip has your vision on you? Does it clutch you with a force that nothing but death can relax, or does it hold you so lightly that you are easily separated from it, discouraged from trying to make it real?

Constant discouragements are a great temptation to abandon one's life dreams, to drop one's standards. One's vision is apt to become blurred in passing through great crises, in periods of general depression, in times of financial stress, but this is really the test of a strong character,—that he does not allow obstacles to divert him from his one aim. The man who is made of the stuff that wins hangs on to his vision, even to the point of starvation, for he knows that there is only one way of bringing it down to earth, and that is by clinging to it through storm and stress, in spite of every obstacle and discouragement.

Never mind what discouragements, misfortunes or failures come to you, let nobody, no combination of unfortunate circumstances, destroy your faith in your dream of what you believe you were made to do. Never mind how the actual facts seem to contradict the results you are after. No matter who may oppose you or how much others may abuse and condemn you, cling to your vision, because it is sacred. It is the God-urge in you. You have no right to allow it to fade or to become dim. Your final success will be measured by your ability to cling to your vision through discouragement. It will depend largely upon your stick-to-it-ive-ness, your bull dog tenacity. If you shrink before criticism and opposition you will demagnetize your mind and lose all the momentum which you have gained in your previous endeavor. No matter how black or threatening the outlook, keep working, keep visualizing your life dream, and some unexpected way will surely open for its fulfillment.

Put out of your mind forever any thought that you can possibly fail in reaching the goal of your longing. Set your face toward it; keep looking steadfastly in the direction of your ambition, whatever it may be; resolve never to recognize defeat, and you will by your mental attitude, your resolution, create a tremendous force for the drawing of your own to you. If you have the grit and stamina to stick, to persevere to the end, if you persistently maintain the victorious attitude toward your vision victory will crown your efforts.

CHAPTER V

A NEW ROSARY

There is a great significance in that passage in St. Mark: "All the things whatsoever ye pray and ask for believe ye have received them and ye have." We are bidden to believe that what we wish has already been fulfilled; that if we take this attitude we shall obtain our desire.

The benefit we derive from prayer is the harmonizing poising, balancing of our own mind, putting ourselves into closer communion into a more vital connection with the Divine Mind, through which we receive a larger supply of our Father's blessings. Prayer is the opening up of the pinched supply pipes of the mind which shut out the divine inflow; it is the letting into our lives greater abundance from the unlimited supply which continually flows from the Source of all sources.

"Mary," said a young girl to a Catholic friend, "why do you carry that rosary everywhere, and what possible good does it do you to count those beads over and over?"

"Oh," answered Mary, "I never could make you understand what a comfort this rosary is to me. When I am tired out, or blue or discouraged about anything; or when I long very much for something that it seems impossible I should ever get, I take my rosary and begin to pray. Before I have gone over half of its beads, everything is changed. The tired, discouraged feeling is gone, or if I have been asking for something I long to have, it doesn't seem nearly so far away as before; and I know that if I don't get just what I ask for, I'll get something better."

Those who are too narrow-minded or too prejudiced to see anything good in a creed which is not their own, often sneer at the Catholic custom of "saying the rosary." To them it is only "superstition," "nonsense," to repeat the same prayer over and over. These people do not understand the philosophy as well as the religion underlying this beautiful old custom. They do not know the power that inheres in the repetition of the spoken word, and in the influence of the thought expressed.

Any one can prove this for himself or herself. It isn't necessary to get a rosary made of beads. You can make your own, an intangible but very real rosary, and if you say it over, not once, or twice a day, but over and over many times, and especially before retiring at night, you will be surprised at the wonderful results.

Is it a fault you wish to correct; is it a talent or gift you desire to develop and improve; is it money, or friends, an education, success in any enterprise; is it contentment, peace of mind, happiness, power to serve, power in your work,—whatever it is you desire, make it a bead in your rosary, pray for its accomplishment, think of it, work for its fulfillment and your desire will materialize.

There are many ways of praying. All our prayers are not vocalized petitions to the Almighty. They are also our inspirations, the aspirations of the soul to be and to do. Desire is prayer. The sincerest prayer may be the longing of the heart to cultivate a talent or talents, or the intense desire to get an education so that one may be of greater service in the world. That which we dream of and struggle to attain, our efforts to make good; these are genuine prayers.

When Jane Addams, as a little girl, longed for the power to lift up other little girls and make them happy; when she dreamed of a time when she should be grown up and doing a great work in the service of humanity, she was praying. She was even then laying the foundations of Hull House, and the Hull House of to-day is an answered prayer. Her whole life from childhood up was a prayer, because it was a preparation for a great and noble work.

When the child, Frances Willard, longed and dreamed in her remote Wisconsin home, she was praying and building as surely as in her later years when she was the moving power of the great organization she had brought into being. "I always wanted to react on the world about me to my utmost ounce of power," she said in telling of her early life and aspirations. "Lying on the prairie grass and lifting my hand toward the sky, I used to say in my inmost spirit, 'What is it? What is the aim to be, O God?'"

Such noble heart yearnings are, in the truest sense, prayers. The uttered prayer clothed in beautiful language, that which is delivered in the pulpit to be heard of men, may not be a real prayer at all. The collective prayer of the congregation may be a mockery. I have often been in churches where people were repeating prayers automatically, while looking all about the auditorium watching other people, mentally occupied, while their lips moved in a so-called prayer, in noticing what they wore and how they looked. There is no real praying in such a performance as this. It is not soul expression, not heart talking. It is mere parrot talking. All mechanical mumbling of prayers in our church services is an insult to the Creator, who does not hear prayers which do not come from the heart.

"Prayer is the heart's sincere desire." What we long for and hope for we pray for by our very longing and hope. The real prayer may be struggling in the heart without words, it may be a noble desire, a heart longing which no language can express. It may be voiceless or it may not, but the true prayer always comes from the heart, and it is always answered.

A remarkable illustration of this is afforded in a story told by John Wesley. He was once riding through a dark wood, carrying with him a large sum of money intrusted to his safe keeping. All at once a sense of fear came over him, and dismounting from his horse, he offered up a prayer for protection. Years afterward Wesley was called to see a dying man. This man told the preacher that at the time he had passed through the wood, so many years before, he, the robber, had been lying in wait to rob him of the money he carried. He told Wesley that he had noticed him dismounting and how, on his remounting and resuming his journey, the appearance of an armed attendant riding beside him had so filled him with awe and a great fear that he had abandoned his purpose.

Balzac said truly: "When we are enabled to pray without weariness, with love, with certainty, with intelligence, we will find ourselves in instant accord with power, and like a mighty roaring wind, like a thunderbolt, our will will cut its way through all things and share the power of God."

Everybody prays, because everybody hopes and desires, has longings and yearnings which he hopes will be realized. In a sense the atheist, the agnostic, the unbeliever, although they may not know it, pray just as much as do believers, for every longing of the heart, every noble aspiration, is a prayer. We pray as naturally as we breathe, for the desire for a better, nobler life, for grander and higher attainment, is an unconscious prayer. Prayer is really our heart hunger for oneness with the Divine, with the Eternal. It is the union of the soul with its Maker. It is literally what Phillips Brooks described it to be, the sluice gate between God and the soul.

Many people mistake the very nature of prayer, and complain that it is no use to pray, because their prayers are never answered.

The reason is clear, and is admirably expressed in Irving Bacheller's pithy verses on "Faith."

"Now, don't expect too much o' God, it wouldn't be quite fair
If fer anything ye wanted ye could only swap a prayer;
I'd pray fer yours, an' you fer mine, an' Deacon Henry Hospur
He wouldn't hev a thing t' do but lay abed an' prosper.
"If all things come so easy, Bill, they'd hev but little worth,
An' some one with a gift o' prayer 'u'd mebbe own the earth.

It's the toil ye give t' git a thing—the sweat an' blood an' care—
That makes the kind o' argument that ought to back yer prayer."

If your prayers come back to you unanswered it is because they are not backed by the conditions on which the answer to prayer depends,—faith and work. You don't get the thing you pray for either because you don't really believe you will get it, or you don't back your prayer with the necessary effort, or because you fail in both requisites.

To pray for a thing and not work for it, not strive and do our level best to obtain it, is a mockery. To ask God to give us that which we long for, but are too lazy to help get ourselves, is begging. In answer to our prayers and longings and efforts we get that which we call out of the universal supply, which is everywhere. Every day some prayer is made visible, something is wrought out of the invisible, manifested in the actual by those two mighty instruments—prayer and work. But if you think your stumbling block will be removed, or your desire realized without raising a finger to help yourself, you may pray until doomsday without ever getting an answer. Prayer without faith is of no avail. And faith without work is a barren virtue.

In the second stanza of a little poem entitled "God's Answer," Ella Wheeler Wilcox gives us the answer to the plaint of the discouraged, unsuccessful soul, who cries that his prayers are not heard, and that no hand is stretched out to lead him to the heights he would attain.

"Then answered God: 'Three things I gave to thee—
Clear brain, brave will and strength of mind and heart,
All implements divine to shape the way;
Why shift the burden of the toil on Me?
Till to the utmost he has done his part
With all his might, let no man dare to pray."

The answer to your prayers is right inside of yourself. They are answered by your obeying the natural as well as the spiritual law of all supply. If you don't do your part in the actual working world down to the minutest detail your prayer is bound to come back to you unanswered.

Everything in the universe has its price, a perfectly legitimate one. You can realize what you desire if you are willing to pay the price, and that is honest, earnest, persistent effort to make it yours. The Creator answers your prayer by fitting you to answer it yourself,

41

by enabling you to put into practice the law of demand and supply, the fundamental principle on which answer to prayer is based. You must put yourself in absolute harmony with the thing you pray for. It cannot be forced. You must attract it. Answer to prayer comes only to a receptive mind in a positive condition, that is, in a condition to create, to achieve.

The law of affirmation and the law of prayer are one and the same. "Affirm that which you wish, work for it, and it will be manifest in your life." Affirm it confidently, with the utmost faith, without any doubt of what you affirm. Say to yourself, "I am that which I think I am—and I can be nothing else." But if you affirm, "I am health; I am prosperity; I am this or that," and do not believe it, you will not be helped by affirmation. You must believe what you affirm; you must constantly strive to be what you assert you are, or your affirmations are but idle breath.

Make yourself a New Thought rosary, not of set formal prayers, but an original one whose beads shall be your heart's aspirations, your desires to e-volve the strong, radiant, successful happy man or woman the Creator has in-volved in you.

If you are unhappy, crushed by repeated failures and disappointment, suffering the pangs of thwarted ambition, put this bead in your rosary and say it over to yourself frequently: "The being God made was never intended for this sort of life. Mary (or John)," addressing yourself by name, "God made you for success, not failure. He never made any one to be a failure. You are perverting the great object of your existence by giving way to discouragement, going about among your fellows with a long, sad, dejected face, as though you were a misfit, as though there were no place for you in this great glad world of abundance. You were made to express gladness, to go through life with a victorious attitude, like a conqueror. The image of God is in you; you must bring it out and exhibit it to the world. Don't disgrace your Maker by violating His image, by being anything but the magnificent man or woman He intended you to be."

Back up every "bead," or prayer you put in your rosary by action during the day, otherwise you might as well save yourself the trouble of stringing your beads, for

"It's the toil ye give t' get a thing—the sweat an' blood an' care—
That makes the kind o' argument that ought to back yer prayer."

Don't be afraid of thinking too highly of yourself, not in the egotistical sense, but because (the Creator having made you in His image) you must have inherited divine qualities, omnipotent possibilities. It is an insult to God to depreciate what He has made and has pronounced good.

If you are a victim of timidity and self-depreciation, afraid to say your soul is your own; if you creep about the world as though you thought you were taking up room which belonged to somebody else; if you shrink from responsibility, from everything which draws attention to yourself; if you are bashful, timid, confused, tongue-tied, when you ought to assert yourself, turn to your rosary and add another bead.

Say to yourself, "I am a child of the King of kings. I will no longer suffer this cowardly timidity to rule me,—a prince of heaven. I am made by the same Creator who has made all other human beings. They are my brothers and sisters. There is no more reason why I should be afraid to express what I feel or think before them than if they were in my own family. I have just as much right on this earth as any potentate, as much right to hold up my head and assert myself as any monarch. I am my Father's heir, and have all the rights of a prince. I have inherited the wealth of the universe. The earth and the stars and the sun are mine. I will quit this everlasting self-depreciation, this self-effacement, this cringing habit of forever appearing to apologize for being alive. It is a crime against my Maker and myself. Henceforth I shall carry myself like a prince. I will act like one, and will walk the earth as a conqueror. I will let no opportunity pass to-day for assuming any responsibility which will enlarge me, for expressing my opinion, for asserting myself whenever and wherever necessary.

"This specter, this shadow of self-depreciation which has held me back so long, which has darkened my path in life must go, for I shall walk henceforth with my face toward the sun so that the shadows of life will fall behind me, and not across my path as before. I am going to face life with a self-respecting, victorious attitude, with a hopeful outlook, for I know that I am victory organized. Here after I am going to think more of myself. I am not going to put myself on the bargain counter any longer by going around as though I had a skim milk opinion of myself. No more of the poorhouse attitude of inferiority for me. I know that I was born for victory, born to conquer. I am going to win out in this great inspiring game of life."

If you feel that you lack initiative, if you are not a self-starter, boldly assert the opposite and add the assertion to your rosary. Stoutly affirm your ability to begin things, to do them as well as they can be done, and to push them through to a complete finish. Learn to trust the God in you. This trust is a divine force which will carry you through. Never again allow yourself to harbor thoughts of your inferiority or deficiency. Say to yourself, "I am going to assert my manhood or womanhood and stand for something. I am going to be a force in the world and not a weakling. I was made to make my life a masterpiece and not a botch; I was created for a great end, and I am going to realize that end. There are forces inside of me which if aroused and put into action would revolutionize my life, and I am going to get control of them, to use them. I am going to find myself and use a hundred per cent. instead of a miserable little fraction of my ability."

If you are obsessed with the idea that you are not as bright, that you have not as much ability as most other people; if you have been called dull, dense, stupid by your parents and teachers, until you have lost confidence in yourself; if you have been dwarfed by the suggestion of inferiority, either through what others have said of you, or the thought you have held of yourself, you must change all this. You must assert your ability and hold tenaciously the ideal of the able, efficient man or woman you long to be and that it is in you to become. You must not only affirm your power to be that which you wish, but you must replace the picture of your inferiority with the ideal of wholeness, of completeness, of the man or woman the Creator intended you to be. Cling to this ideal of yourself, assert your superiority, and you will soon drive out the dwarfed, inferior, defective image which others, or your own false thoughts, have established in your subconsciousness. Holding the truth, the perfect ideal, in mind will give you confidence, assurance to do the thing you are capable of doing.

Thousands of students have failed to pass examinations not because of inability to answer test questions, but because of fear, loss of self-confidence engendered by the blighting suggestion of inferiority. This is especially true of highstrung, sensitive natures.

If you brood over the failure suggestion, if you visualize an inferior picture of yourself, you will become obsessed with the failure idea, with the thought of your inefficiency, and make it wellnigh impossible for you to succeed in any undertaking. If for any reason you have dropped into the failure habit, you will have to make a very determined effort to break away from it, or your life will indeed be a failure.

I know a young man who is both efficient and ambitious, but when the opportunity for which, perhaps, he has been working a long time comes, he wilts. His courage fails and he does not feel equal to it. He can see how somebody else can do the thing required, but he fears it is too much for him. He has never done anything like it before; and he is afraid to make the attempt because he might fail.

Now, if you feel this way about yourself, just add another bead to your rosary. Cut "I can't" out of your vocabulary and substitute "I can,"—for he can who thinks he can. Napoleon, one of the greatest achievers the world has ever seen, hated the word "can't" and would never use it if it could be avoided. He did not believe in the "impossible." When he was praised for his daring and genius in crossing the Alps in the dead of winter, he said, "I deserve no credit except for refusing to believe those who said it could not be done."

Did you ever think that every time you say "I can't" you weaken your confidence in yourself and your power to do things? Did you ever know a person who has a great many "I cant's," and excuses in his vocabulary to accomplish very much? Some people are always using the words, "Oh, I can't do that;" "I can't afford this;" "I can't afford to go there;" "I can't undertake such a hard task, let somebody else do that." These negative assertions undermine power. Have nothing to do with them. In all questions of achievement, let your rosary deal in affirmations. Instead of "I can't," say "I can," "I must," "I will." Begin what you fear to undertake, and half its difficulties will vanish.

If you are vexed, worried, and like Martha, "troubled about many things;" if you are suffering from all sorts of discord; if you are not feeling well, you will get great comfort from turning to your rosary and repeating some of the blessed Biblical promises. "Neither shall any plagues (discord or harm) come nigh thy dwelling. This is the promise to him that dwelleth in the secret place of the Most High. I will restore health into thinking and I will heal thee of thy wounds." "He that dwelleth in the secret place of the Most High shall abide under the shadow of the Almighty," "The Lord is my refuge, my fortress. In Him will I trust." "Thou shalt not be afraid of the terror by night, nor for the arrow that flieth by day," "Surely He shall deliver thee from the snare of the fowler, from the pestilence that walketh in darkness," "He shall cover thee with his feathers, and under his wings shalt thou trust."

The contemplation of God and the frequent repetition of these beautiful Bible passages will increase your faith and your consciousness of oneness with the Infinite.

Make it a rule never to affirm of your health, your success, or yourself what you do not wish to be true. Don't say that you feel "rocky," that you are used up, played out, that you feel miserable, that you don't feel like doing anything. Never tell people of your aches and pains, for every repetition means etching the black

45

pictures of these conditions deeper and deeper into your consciousness. Instead of thus intensifying them, say to yourself, "The Power that created, and that sustains me every instant of my life, repairs, renews, restores, cures me. I am health, I am vigor, I am power, I am that which I think I am." Refuse to see or to hold for an instant an imperfect, discordant sin or disease-marred image of yourself. Do not harbor a suggestion of your inferiority, physically or mentally. Always picture yourself as a great, strong, splendid man or woman, clean, true, beautiful—a sublime specimen of humanity. Do not allow yourself to harbor a thought of physical or mental weakness. Think health, power, perfection at every breath. Persist in holding the thought of yourself as you long to be, the ideal which your Creator saw ahead of you when he fashioned you. Cling to your vision of health without taint, weakness or defect.

Have you a hair-trigger temper, and do you fly all to pieces over the least provocation, starting raging fires in your brain that are as destructive to your mental and physical forces as are the great forest fires to the vast tracts of territory over which they sweep? If you have you are minimizing all your powers and seriously endangering your success, your happiness, your life itself. Ask Sing Sing what the hot tempers, the fires of uncontrolled anger, of jealous rage, of revenge, of hate, of all the explosive passions have done. Ask the poorhouses, the insane asylums, the morgues, ask the records of human wreckage everywhere, what the fruits of uncontrolled passions of every sort are.

Anger, whatever its cause, is temporary insanity. Are you in the habit of losing your temper, of flying into a rage over trifles? If you could only see what a miserable spectacle, what a fool exhibition, you make of yourself on such occasions, when you go all to pieces and rave like a madman because you miss your train, or because you think some one insults you, when you step down from the throne of your reason and let the brute sit there and rule in your place, you would be so chagrined and mortified that you would leave nothing undone to rid yourself of your fault. Why, nothing could hire you, when in your right mind, to make such a ludicrous and contemptible exhibition of yourself. You only do it when under the stress of angry passion, when shorn of your power by this temporary insanity.

To retain self-control, mental poise, equanimity, under all provocations, great or small, is an index of a fine strong character. It is a triumph of strength over weakness, of greatness over littleness. The habit of conquering ourselves is the habit of victory; it strengthens all the faculties.

46

You can bring this great force of control to your aid, by calling on the divinity within you, by asserting your oneness with the Divine who is eternal calmness. Say to yourself, "God's image is in me. I am of divine lineage. I was not intended to be passion's slave. It is unworthy of a real man, of a real woman, to be the plaything of temper, or any sort of explosive tearing down passion. There is something divine in me and I will not allow my lower nature to get control."

The constant affirmation of your oneness with your Creator, with the One, will give you a wonderful sense of power, and will help you to overcome every handicap. But you must be very positive, very insistent and persistent in your affirmations. No matter what fault you are trying to overcome or what good quality you are anxious to acquire there must be no weakness, indecision or vacillation in your affirmations or your efforts.

If you are cursed with the fatal habit of indecision; if you are a weak vacillator, always taking things up for reconsideration because you are not quite sure that you have done the right thing; if you allow yourself to waver, to doubt the wisdom of your decision, you will be incapable of ever under any circumstances arriving at an intelligent conclusion.

You can cure the curse of indecision by asserting your power to see clearly, think quickly and act decisively. If you are in doubt as to what career to choose; if you hesitate in regard to what course you should take in any difficulty, which of two or three paths you should follow, whatever your problem may be, ask for light and the divine power within will come to your aid and guide you aright. Repeat the "I am" in every instance. "I am positive." "I can decide vigorously, firmly, finally." Resolve every morning that you will, during that day, decide things without possibility of recall or reconsideration. First go over the matter to be decided very thoroughly and carefully. In making your decision use the best judgment at your command and then close the incident. You will secure yourself against vacillation by refusing, after it is thus closed, to wonder whether you have done the wisest thing, by resisting every temptation to open the matter for reconsideration.

If you feel that you are a coward somewhere in your nature, you can strengthen this deficient faculty wonderfully by holding the courageous ideal, by thinking and reading about heroic people and things, holding the thought of fearlessness, that you are God's child, that you are not afraid of anything on the earth. Study the stories of heroic lives; think, act, live, the heroic thought. Say, "I am a son of God, and I was never made to cower, to slink, to be afraid. Fear is

47

not an attribute of divinity. I am brave, courageous; I am a conqueror."

If you are suffering with the poverty disease, if your whole life has been stunted by poverty, saturated with poverty-stricken thoughts and convictions, if you have been heading towards the poverty goal, just turn about face, and put the law of abundance into operation. Face towards prosperity and success instead of poverty and failure. All the good things you need are yours by inheritance. Claim them, expect them, work for them, pray for them, and you will realize them in your life. Make this last stanza of Ella Wheeler Wilcox's splendid little poem "Assertion" a new bead on your rosary. Repeat it frequently, and work cheerfully, confidently, courageously toward its fulfillment.

> *"I am success. Though hungry, cold, ill-clad,*
> *I wander for a while. I smile and say,*
> *'It is but for a time—I shall be glad*
> *To-morrow, for good fortune comes my way.*
> *God is my father, He has wealth untold,*
> *His wealth is mine, health, happiness and gold."*

If you have made fatal mistakes for which you have been ostracized from society; if you are morbidly worrying over some unfortunate experience, thus making it bigger, blacker and more hideous, just thrust it out of your mind, bury it, forget it, say to it, "You have no power over me; I will not allow you to destroy my peace and thwart my career; you are not the truth of my being; the reality of me is divine, and you cannot touch that. I can and I will rise above all my troubles, make good all my mistakes and errors. From now on I will work with the God in me. I will not be overcome. I will overcome."

If you are the slave of a demon habit which has blasted your hopes, blighted your happiness, thwarted your ambition, cast its black shadow across your whole life, say to yourself: "I will break away from this vile habit. I will be free and not a slave."

If it is impurity, say, "I was not made to be dominated by such a monstrous vice. God's image in me was not intended to wallow in this filth. I have suffered long enough from this damnable habit, which is undermining my health, killing my chances of success in life, and lowering me below the level of the beast. I am a child of the Infinite, sent here to make a worthy contribution to humanity, to make good. I am going to make good. I am going to free myself from this base habit and recover my self-respect, my manhood, at any cost. I am going to be a MAN, not a THING, a son of God, not of the devil."

Continually flood your mind with purity thoughts and affirmations which will neutralize your sensual desires. Repeat again and again your determination not to allow your life to be spoiled by unrestrained passion. Make such an emphatic and vigorous call upon your better self, make the demand so appealing that your higher nature will be aroused and will dominate your acts. Say, "The Creator has bidden me look up, not down. He made me to climb, not to descend and wallow in the mire of animalism."

If it is drink, opium, excessive smoking, or any other vicious habit that is robbing you of manhood and holding you back in life, string this bead on your rosary, "I was not made to be dominated by you, a mere weed, an extract of grain, a habit which I forged. I am done with you once and forever. The appetite for you is destroyed. There is something divine within me which makes me perfectly able to overcome you. You are a vile thing, and have disgraced me for the last time. Never again can you humiliate me and make me despise myself. There can be only one ruler in my mental kingdom and I propose to be that one. I don't propose to allow you Whiskey, Cigarette, Opium, or other Drug or Devil, to ruin my life, to force me to carry in my face the signs of my defeat, the scarlet letter of my degradation, my failure. You have humiliated, insulted me, tyrannized over me long enough, making me confess that I hadn't enough strength of mind to stand up against a single vicious, degrading habit. Now I defy you. Your power over me is at an end. The spell is broken. Hereafter I am going to walk the earth as a conqueror, a victor, not as a slave. I am going to front the world with my head up and face forward. God and one make a majority. I am in the majority NOW."

There is no inferiority or depravity about the man God made. No matter how low you may have fallen, the God image in you never can be smirched or depraved. It is as perfect in the worst criminal in the penitentiary as it is in the greatest saint. There is something in every human being that is incontaminable, something which is never sick, never diseased, and which never sins. This is the God in us, and herein lies the hope of the most brutal human being on the earth. There is something in him that is divine, sinless, immortal, the God in him which when called will instantly rush to his aid.

If you feel that you have wandered very far from your God, that you had gotten out of the current which runs Heavenward, just repeat to yourself such things as this, "Nearer My God to Thee, Nearer to Thee." This will help you to put up your trolley pole, to make your connection with the Divine wire which carries omnipotent power. The sense of separateness will disappear and the load under which you staggered before will grow light, will be lifted from you.

The secret of all health, prosperity, happiness, power, love, of victorious living, is a consciousness of union, of oneness with the Divine. This is the secret of all human blessedness. When you are in this Godward current you are "nearer to God," and you cannot fear, for you know that no harm can come to infinite power.

The closer we are to divinity, the greater our strength and efficiency. What makes us weak and inefficient is that we have shut off this power by our wrong thinking, vicious living. Your life will take on a new meaning, a diviner dignity, when you consciously realize your at-one-ment with the great creative, sustaining Principle of the universe.

Nothing will be of more help to you in achieving this great result than the constant daily use of your New Thought rosary. It will help you to put further and further away the things that make you weak, that make you think you are a mere puppet, at the mercy of a cruel Fate, which tosses you about in the world regardless of your own birthright, desires, and volition. You can make each bead a prayer, an affirmation, to lead you closer and closer to the Source of all things. Whether it be the overcoming of a vicious habit, the strengthening of some defect or deficiency, the getting away from poverty and despair, whatever you desire, you can repeat your affirmation concerning it, silently, if with others, audibly when you are alone, until it becomes a part of you. Especially repeat the beads of your rosary which fit your greatest needs before retiring to sleep.

If you have been demagnetizing yourself, neutralizing your hopes, your ambition and your efforts by your black, vicious outlook upon life, by your doubts, and worries, your fear of poverty, of sickness, of misfortune, of death, put these things out of your mind, and say, "God is my helper. God is my supply, I cannot want. God is my shepherd, I cannot lack. I must live in full realization of my oneness with Infinite Life."

Each one of us is a part of the living God and we are powerful, victorious and happy just in proportion as we realize our oneness with Him, and weak, abject and miserable just in the degree we separate ourselves from Him, the All-Source, the All-Supply.

CHAPTER VI

ATTRACTING THE POORHOUSE

As long as you hold the poorhouse thought you are heading toward the poorhouse. A pinched, stingy thought means a pinched, stingy reply.

No matter how hard one may work, if he constantly holds the poverty ideal, the poorhouse thought in his mind, he is driving away the very thing he is pursuing.

The man who sows failure thoughts, poverty thoughts, can no more reap success, prosperity harvests, than a farmer can get a wheat crop from sowing thistles.

Poverty is a mental disease.

Some one has said that no one ever went to the poorhouse who did not attract the poorhouse by his poorhouse mental attitude. Observation and long study of the question have convinced me that, as a rule, people who make miserable failures of their lives expected to do so. They had such a horror of the poorhouse, they lived in such terror of coming to want, that they shut off the very source of their supply. They had so warped their minds that they could see nothing ahead but poverty. They wasted the precious energy which might have been utilized in happiness and prosperity building, in expecting, dreading and preparing for the dire things that might come upon them, and, according to the law, they got what they dreaded and feared.

Thinking war, talking war, anticipating it, getting ready for it, in other words, preparedness for war, the perpetual war suggestion, was largely responsible for the outbreak of the greatest war in history. If all the nations involved had talked peace, thought peace, expected it, prepared for it, there would have been peace, not war.

So long as people talk poverty, think poverty, expect it, get ready for it, they will have poverty. Preparedness for poverty, expecting it, attracts it, confirms poverty conditions.

We are constantly drawing to ourselves that which we expect. If you are sending out a perpetual poverty thought current, a doubt current, a discouragement current, no matter how hard you may be working in the opposite direction, you will never get away from the current you set in motion. The sort of thought current you generate will flow back to you.

Everywhere we see people trying hard to get on, struggling early and late to better their condition, and yet never expecting, or even hoping to be prosperous. They do not believe they are going to get what they are working for, and they do not.

A typical example of those who keep themselves in the poverty current is a woman I know who is constantly affirming her inability to better her condition. She answers her better-off friends who tell her that she ought to have this and that by saying, "Oh, it is all very well for you rich folks to talk this way, but these things are not for me. We have always been poor and I suppose we always shall be; we can only have the bare necessities of life, and are fortunate if we get these. Of course I might indulge in a little treat for myself and the children now and then, but that would be extravagant, and I must save for a rainy day."

Now, I have no quarrel with people who save for a rainy day. It is the part of prudence to be prepared for all emergencies. It is a splendid thing to save for spending, for enjoyment in our later years, but people who begin early to provide for the "rainy day," and who deny themselves every little pleasure and enjoyment for the sake of adding to this provision, fall into the habit of pinching themselves, and usually continue to do so through life.

This woman limits her supply by her conviction that every cent she can spare must go to the rainy day fund because she is always going to be poor. She assures herself and others that she is never going to have the things she would like to have, because of her poverty, and so she starves the lives of herself and her boy and girl in anticipating a day of possible want. She is a type of a multitude of men and women who settle down to their poverty, become half reconciled to its limitations, and do not make a strenuous effort to get away from it. That is, they never dream of exercising their creative, positive thought, but continue to live and to realize in their conditions the negative, destructive, poverty thought.

These are the people who are always saying they "cannot afford" things. They cannot afford to send the boy or girl to school or college this year. They cannot afford the necessary clothes or the needed vacation because of the rainy day, which, like a specter, rises at every feast, on every occasion when they try to get some enjoyment or satisfaction out of the present. They are always postponing things till next year. But this "next year" never comes, and the children never go to the academy or college, and they themselves never take the needed vacation, the travel in one's own country or the long promised trip abroad. They keep forever postponing the enjoyment of the good things of life until they can "afford it;" and that time never comes for people of this apprehensive habit of mind, because they always want to lay up a little more for the future.

I know a number of people well along in years who are still pinching themselves not only on the comforts but even on the necessities of life in anticipation of the possible rainy day, for which they are always planning. They make life one long continuous rainy day, and little realize that they often tend to create the need for which they are perpetually saving.

We sometimes read in newspapers striking illustrations of the results of this starved, rainy day habit of mind. A New York daily recently reported a typical instance; that of an aged woman who had died alone in the slums of the metropolis. She had been dead several days when her body was found, and so wretched were her surroundings, it was at first supposed that she was penniless. On investigation, however, it was found that the woman had had in ready cash and in bank deposits, almost ten thousand dollars.

Pauperized by her diseased mind, this wretched creature, like many another poverty-stricken soul, died of starvation in the midst of plenty. Her mind was so obsessed with the poverty thought that she even denied herself the necessities of life. For years she had shut herself away from the great stream of life flowing all around her, so that she might hoard, and hoard, and hoard. She would allow no one to enter her rooms, and died alone and uncared for, leaving behind her the money which would have made her comfortable, happy, useful, and would have prolonged her life. She was as truly a victim of the poverty disease as though she didn't have a cent.

The children of Israel while passing through the wilderness were constantly reflecting the poverty thought,—"Can God furnish for us a table in the wilderness? Of course not, it is not reasonable. We shall starve if we do not get back to Egypt." But for the faith of their great leader, Moses, in the Power that led them, they would have gone back to Egypt, back to the slavery and poverty from which they had fled. Even after the manna had been given them fresh every day for a long time, they did not believe the supply would continue. They were still skeptical and tried to store enough manna for "a rainy day," but it would not keep and they were forced to trust to a new supply every day.

"But where is our supply coming from? How are we going to pay the rent, the mortgage off the home, the farm? Where is the money coming from? What will happen to us if we cannot get it? Where are the children's clothes coming from? How are we going to get the necessaries of life? Where is our supply coming from? Why can't I get a job that will enable us to really live?" These are the questions multitudes of people all over the world are asking themselves. They express the acuteness of the suffering from the poverty disease, so apparent in every civilized country.

Nothing else gives human beings so much anxiety, nothing else is such a perpetual irritant as this fear of what is coming in the future, this dread of poverty, of not being able to provide for the necessities and the comforts of those dear to us, the fear of not being able to maintain ourselves and to rear our children in comfort and respectability. It demagnetizes us, drives away the things we want and draws to us those we dread. Job said, "The thing I greatly feared has come upon me"—that which I was afraid of has come to me. People who have an abnormal fear of poverty attract the very condition they dread and are trying to get away from, because the mind relates with whatever it dwells on. Our doubts and hatreds and fears; the thing we relate with, we attract.

Whatever you allow your mind to dwell on, you are unconsciously creating. If you think continually of misfortunes, of poverty; if you fear you are going to fail in your work, that you may come to want; if you are always thinking about the possibility of your business declining; if you fear you are losing your grip on your trade or profession, you are aggravating your trouble and making it worse and worse. There are multitudes of people who never expect even to be comfortable, to say nothing of having luxuries. They expect poverty, hard times, and do not understand that this very expectancy increases their magnetic power to attract what they do not want.

Not long ago a young man who was greatly depressed because he could not get on in the world, asked me what I thought the trouble was. He said he had always worked hard, but did not seem to make any headway. About all he could do was to earn a bare living. Everything appeared to go against him. Fate, he complained, seemed determined to keep him down, no matter how hard he might struggle against it, and he was doomed to be poor, to be a nobody. He believed that hard luck, poverty and failure were family traits; for his father and grandfather, he said, were hard workers too, but they could never get on, never get away from poverty, and he didn't expect he ever would either.

Another, an older man, who sought my advice in a similar difficulty, lamented the fearful inequality of human conditions, and railed against his luck and the injustice of fate. "I work early and late, Sundays and holidays," he said, "and haven't taken a vacation for years. I have been struggling and striving and pushing to make my way in the world since I was a boy, and here I am past fifty and have never succeeded in anything yet. Now there is something wrong somewhere in society when such persistence and such constant efforts do not enable one to get anywhere, or to rise to any position worth while."

I asked him about his early training and education. He acknowledged that he had not made much of a preparation for his life work, because, he said, his father also had been a tremendous worker, had always tried hard to better his condition but like himself had never succeeded, and so he had come to the conclusion that success was not in the family, and that it was no use to spend years in preparing for a career, for there was no chance that very much would come to him anyway.

These two are types of people who are constantly heading toward poverty and failure in their minds, and then complaining when they have got what they invited. By the law of mental attraction they could not get anything but poverty and failure. Each had desired success and prosperity but had always expected the opposite. He had slaved and toiled in an aimless sort of way, belittling himself and his talents, with the inner belief that it was all he was good for anyway, and that if success by any chance ever came his way it would be a stroke of luck, and not because it was his due by inherent right.

No man can become prosperous as long as he holds in his mind the picture of limitation, of lack and want. We do not get things in this world which we do not believe we can get. We do not accomplish what we doubt we can do, even though we have the ability to do it.

I knew a boy in college who always felt certain he was going to fail in his examinations, and he did fail invariably. Yet it was due more to his fear, his terror, of failure than to a lack of ability or preparation in his studies. He had formed a habit of expecting failure, of predicting misfortunes, of looking and preparing for them, and so far as I know they have followed him through life.

In every community, in every occupation and profession, there are able, conscientious men and women who try very hard, so far as their actual labor is concerned, to get on in the world, but who don't expect to get on. It is pitiful to see them toiling day after day, but always facing in the wrong direction. They are working for success in their vocations, working for a competence for themselves and their families, but all the time expecting failure, anticipating poverty, living in an atmosphere of mental penury.

There is no law of philosophy by which you can possibly produce

55

just the opposite of what you are holding in your mind, what you are concentrating on. If you are thinking down, if you are afraid, are worried, if you have fears and doubts, if you keep visualizing, thinking, talking hard times, panics and financial crises, your business will shrink and shrivel accordingly. If, on the other hand, you have confidence, expectation of better things, if you are convinced that conditions are going to improve, you set in motion a thought current that will back your efforts with an irresistible force. But a thought current saturated with the fear of failure, with doubts and discouragement will neutralize your most strenuous efforts.

Instead of starting on their active careers with the victorious attitude, with the idea that their careers are to be a triumphal march, many, if not the majority of youths, begin with the impression that they are not victory organized. This is because they have lived in a failure atmosphere, and have absorbed the poverty idea. They have been reared with the fear of failure in their minds, a dread of poverty, a terror of coming to want.

Write it in your heart that a beneficent Creator, who planned a universe full of good things for our use and enjoyment, never meant that we should starve or be miserable. If we are unsuccessful, unhappy, it is because of our attitude toward God and life. Most of us assume the position of beggars instead of that of children of an all-powerful Father, and we remain beggars to the end.

One of the worst things about being very poor is the danger of becoming reconciled to penury, expecting it, holding the conviction that we shall always be poor, that there is no help for it. The habit of thinking we must remain poor because we are so is a paralyzing habit.

Whatever we have accustomed ourselves to for any length of time tends to become a fixed mode of life. Multitudes of people have become so accustomed to their poverty environment, so used to taking it for granted that they are going to remain poor, that they do not take the necessary steps to get away from poverty; and they do not even know that the first step must be a mental one. Instead of this they are all the time affirming their poverty, getting more and more deeply imbedded in the poverty condition by their poverty thoughts and convictions.

The early years of multitudes of children are saturated with the poverty suggestion. They breathe a poverty atmosphere. They hear poverty talk perpetually. They acquire a poverty vocabulary. Their fathers and mothers are always talking poverty, bemoaning their hard conditions, complaining that they were born poor, and must die poor. Children reared in such a mental environment get a sort of poverty habit from which it is very difficult to get away.

The facing toward poverty and despair, heading toward hopelessness and failure, is the worst thing about poverty. The fixity of their conviction that they cannot get away from poverty, their resignation to it, their firm belief that they can never rise into prosperity,—these are the most distressing things about the very poor. There is a tremendous difference between the prospects as well as the mental attitude and the facial expression of a poor boy on a farm who dreams of the day when he can go to college, who pictures himself there, who believes with all his heart that his dream will be realized, and the prospects, the mental attitude and face of another boy similarly situated, who also longs for an education, but has abandoned all hope of ever going to college, or ever getting away from the grinding drudgery and monotony of the farm which he hates.

We must change our thought before we can change our conditions. The thought always leads in any achievement. It would be as impossible for the great mass of poor people to improve their position materially while holding their present mental attitude, the persistent belief that they are always going to be poor, and that they never can do what others have done to get out of their rut, as it would be for the boy who longs to go to college, but who has made up his mind that it is impossible, to get a higher education. While they think that all others are lucky and they are unlucky, while they continue talking about their hard fate and thinking that the rich are getting all the good things of the world and that they are getting only the dregs and never will get anything else, why, of course they will never get anything else.

Most poor people have about the same attitude toward poverty that those who are constantly ailing have toward health. Habitual invalids never expect to be really well. They are always anticipating the development of some disease, looking for the symptoms, imagining that they are going to have this or that physical disability or disease. The way to have health is to think it, to expect it, to visualize it, to realize that health is a positive everlasting fact, and disease only negation, the absence of health, which is brought about largely by a wrong mental attitude, by self-thought poisoning, by disobeying the laws of health. If we are going to be well, we must think vigorous, robust, cheerful, health thoughts, and we must observe the laws of health. We shall have the same degree of health that we give to our mental health model. It is our visualizing of health that brings the expected condition. It is the same with poverty.

Not long ago a poor man told me he would be perfectly satisfied if he could be assured that he would never have to go to the poorhouse, that he would have enough to provide the bare necessities for his little family. He said he never expected to have anything better. He was satisfied that it was not intended for him to have any luxuries. He had always been a poor man, and he always expected to be poor.

Now, this is just the thing that kept this man poor, for he was a hard worker. He al ways expected to be poor. He did not expect anything better. He merely worked for the bare necessities of life, did not expect anything else, and of course he only just managed to squeeze along, making but a bare subsistence. This attitude of the poor toward poverty tends to increase it, to aggravate their disease. So long as one holds the poverty thought he is making himself a poverty magnet, and continually drawing to himself unfortunate conditions.

We have a good illustration of this, a real object lesson, in the grayhaired men everywhere seeking a job. I have watched these desperate men on their rounds looking for work. They are poverty stricken in appearance; their expression is one of utter hopelessness. They look like men who are going downhill, men who have reached the period of diminishing returns, and they feel exactly as they look. Their appearance is the reflex of their thought. Their dress, their manner, their gait, the look in their eyes, everything about them corresponds to their mental attitude, and all point downgrade.

If these men would only brace up, look up, dress up, before they seek a job, there would be some hope for them. If they can't get better clothes they can brush the old ones, blacken their shoes, have a bath and shave, and above all a mental clean-up, and their chances will be ten to one compared with what they were before their physical and mental clean-up.

A man has got to radiate confidence in himself, the expectation of success, before he can get a job. He has got to show that he has reserve power, that there is a lot of good blood in him, working material, success possibilities, or nobody will want him. The man who goes to an employer in a discouraged attitude and begs for work on the ground that he needs it very much; who whines and complains how hard it is for any one who shows the signs of age to get a job, is not going to get one.

If you are in the clutches of a poverty so dire that it robs you even of the desire to get away from it, you are cursed with self-thought poisoning. This is what mars and embitters so many lives, drives away happiness, health and prosperity.

Poverty is usually a disease. It is just as much a disease as is smallpox or tuberculosis. It is just as abnormal to the human being

58

as any disease of the flesh. So is failure. Fear, worry, anxiety, these are all mental diseases, from which few human beings seem to escape. But we are gradually finding an antitoxin for the virus of those diseases so fatal to efficiency, health, happiness and prosperity.

The Bible tells us "The destruction of the poor is their poverty." Every investigator of slum life in our big cities, every record of the lives of the unfortunate poor in our midst proves that this is an absolute truth.

Extreme poverty is a scourge that draws its victims down from depths to lower depths; that makes life a bitter struggle for the bare crumbs that hold body and soul together. When these are not forthcoming it drives the weak, despairing struggler to crime in order to keep himself from starving, or if he is still too proud to steal, to beg, or to go to the poorhouse he ends his life, rather than wait for the slow cruel process of starvation to quench it out. Every year poverty claims its tens of thousands of innocent victims among the little children who die of disease and neglect in damp, foul cellars where the sun never enters. It sweeps them into mills and factories where, robbed of the rights of childhood, they become warped and twisted men and women, full of bitterness, discontent, unrest and unsatisfied ambitions and longings. It drives multitudes to crime, to insanity, to death. In short, poverty is responsible for more ignorance and crime, more discontent and unhappiness, more suicides and ruined ambitions, more wrecked hopes and homes than almost anything else. Verily "the destruction of the poor is their poverty."

If we are to progress as a race, as a civilization, we must, emphatically, drive this crushing poverty disease from our midst. Instead of lauding its blessings, as some do, it is our duty to get away from it, and to help others to do so.

The poverty disease, the poverty curse, is not a decree of Providence. It is largely the result of ignorance. Every human being on this earth could be living in comfort if they knew the powers locked up in themselves and were willing to work and make the best use of them. If the poverty antidotes were as generally known as are the poison antidotes there would be no poor people.

Human beings in the aggregate are in much the same position regarding the poverty antitoxin as the medical profession in regard to newly discovered antitoxin for some terrible disease. Physicians do not know how to apply it safely and effectively, and until practice has established its great value its use is limited. When the knowledge and the use of the poverty remedy become general the disease will be conquered.

As the race becomes more intelligent and better educated we eliminate a multitude of conditions to which people formerly thought they were born, and that there was no escape from them. Many evils which have been conquered by science and education were at one time regarded as scourges sent by God to punish us for our sins, to chasten us. Diseases which struck terror to the hearts of human beings a hundred years ago, and from which they fled in horror, are not feared at all to-day. Intelligence and science have mastered the great plagues which in the Middle and Dark Ages carried off their terrified victims by the million. We have no fear of those plagues to-day, because we have obliterated their causes. We know now that the prevention of those frightful epidemics is merely a matter of sanitation, scientific hygiene, intelligent, healthful living. We know that they were scourges forged by ignorance and not "judgments" of God.

Is it not reasonable to believe that, having conquered so many of the enemies of the race by intelligent thought and scientific methods, we can conquer them all by similar means? Poverty is a plague, a mental disease which can be conquered by intelligent scientific methods. We know its causes and we can remove them. They are largely mental.

It is not necessary to call in a physician to treat the poverty disease. The sufferer can be his own physician. He can heal himself. If you are afflicted with the disease, and want to know how to get rid of it, read the next chapter.

CHAPTER VII

MAKING YOURSELF A PROSPERITY MAGNET

Though culture is the most important business of life. The habit of claiming as our own, as a vivid, present reality that which we desire with all our heart, is a magnetic power which attracts the things we long for. The more persistently we hold the prosperity thought, the more we strengthen and intensify it, the more we increase its power to attract prosperity.

Thinking abundance, visualizing prosperity, will open up the mind, and set the thought currents toward increased supply.

We are so made that about all we get in life is the reflex of what first flows out from us. Whatever thought you send out will draw to you in the material world a corresponding reality.

Every human being is a magnet, the attractive power of which may be developed in any desired direction. Each one can so direct this power that he can draw to himself whatever he wills.

Before your life can be really effective you must make yourself a magnet for the things that will make it so. You must learn how to attract, how to draw to yourself all that will help you to succeed in your work, that will enable you to attain your ambitions.

If poverty is holding you down, you can conquer it by making yourself a prosperity magnet. We are living in the midst of a stream of inexhaustible supply. It is one's own fault if he does not take from this stream whatever he needs.

What we get in life we get by the law of attraction. Like attracts like. Whatever you may have managed to get together in this world you have attracted by your mentality. You may say that you have earned these things, that you have bought them with your salary, the fruit of your endeavor. True, but your thought preceded your endeavor. Your mental plan went before your achievement.

The mere changing of your mental attitude will very soon begin to change conditions. Your decision to face toward prosperity hereafter, to cultivate it, to make yourself a prosperity magnet will tend to draw to you the things that will satisfy your ambition.

The text "He that hath a bountiful eye shall be blessed" is the expression of a fundamental truth. The pictures you make in your mind's eye, the thoughts you harbor are day by day building your outward conditions. They are real forces working ceaselessly in the unseen, and the more you think and visualize favorable conditions the more you increase your power to realize them. You make yourself a magnet for the thing you desire. This is a psychological law.

If you want to become a prosperity magnet you must not only think prosperity but you must also turn your back resolutely on poverty. Begin to-day. Don't wait for to-morrow or next day. If you don't look prosperous, assume a prosperous appearance. Dress as far as possible like a prosperous man or woman, walk like one, act like one, think in terms of prosperity. A mental healer could not cure a cancer by holding in his mind a picture of the hideous disease, with all its horrible appearances and symptoms. He must eliminate all this from his mind. He must see his patient whole, clean, healthy, just as God intended him to be, free from all disease. He must picture to himself the ideal man, and declare his divinity.

The same thing is true in curing yourself of poverty. You can not do this as long as you hold poverty-stricken conditions in your mind. If you want to be prosperous you must hold the prosperous thought, the prosperous picture in your mind. You must refuse to see or recognize poverty. You must not acknowledge it in your manner. You must erase all marks of it, not only from your mental attitude, but just as far as possible from your appearance. Even if you are not able to wear fine clothes at first, or to live in a fine house, you can radiate the hope and expectancy of the glorious inheritance which is your birthright, and everything about you will reflect this light.

Prosperity begins in the mind. You must lay its foundations in your thoughts, surround yourself with a prosperity atmosphere. In other words, you will build into your environment, into your life, whatever dwells in your mind.

We hear of some people that "they are always lucky"; "everything seems to come their way." Things come their way because there are invisible thought forces radiating from their minds toward the goal they have set for themselves. Things fall in line and come our way just in proportion to the force and velocity of the thought forces we project.

Thinking better things might be called the first aid to the poor. To picture yourself as prosperous, living in a comfortable home, wearing good clothes, surrounded with the refinements of life, in a position to do your best work in the service of mankind, this is to put yourself into the current that runs successward.

It is a strange thing that most of us believe the Creator will help us in everything but our financial troubles. We seem to think that it is in some way almost sacrilegious to call upon Him for money to meet our needs. We may ask for comfort, for solace in our afflictions, for the assuaging of our griefs and the healing of our diseases, but to implore God to help us to pay the rent, to pay off the mortgage on the home or the farm, does not seem quite right.

Yet we know perfectly well that every mouthful of food we eat, the material for the clothing we wear and for the houses we live in, every breath we breathe must come from this Divine Source, of infinite supply. If the sun were to be blotted out, or to cease to send its magic rays to the earth, in a few days there would not be a single living thing on the globe. Not a human being, not an animal could exist without it. Not a tree, not a plant, not a flower, no fruits, no vegetables, no grass, nothing green, no vegetable life would be possible. Without the sun's energizing power all life would cease on this planet. It would be as cold, barren and lifeless as on the moon. The Creator is the builder and provider of the universe. Everything we have comes from Him, and without the supply which flows from His abundance we could not live a single instant, and why should we not look to this great Source for our money supply?

The truth is we were all intended to live the life abundant. The Creator never meant His children to grovel in poverty, to spend their lives in drudgery and uncertainty. They have a right to their inheritance of all that is good and beautiful, all that is needful for their welfare. We were not intended to live the pinched, starved, stunted lives of paupers. It is our own fault if we do. The door to opulence is open to every human being born into this world, and no one but himself can close that door. No human being can shut out the lowliest child that is born from his divine inheritance. The only real poverty is in the mind, and no one can control one's mind but himself.

Never for a moment harbor the thought that anything can come to you but prosperity, for this is your birthright; and because it is, you should demand it. Instead of admitting poverty say to yourself, "I am in the midst of abundance. I lack nothing that I need because my Father is the Infinite Source."

Turn your back on poverty. Make up your mind that you will never again have anything to do with it, that you will not encourage it by dwelling on and visualizing poverty suggestions. Face toward prosperity. Think of, and plan for prosperous conditions; struggle toward prosperity with all your might and you will draw it to you.

Suppose you are poor and live in a humble home, just have a talk with your wife and children, and make up your minds that you will all focus on your objective—improved conditions,—that you will face the other way, toward prosperity instead of poverty. Say to yourself, "It is a shame for God's children to exhibit such a pauperized appearance. It is a reflection on my Father-Mother-God to go about among my fellows looking as though everything had gone wrong with me, as though I were disappointed with life. This is ungrateful. I can at least show gratitude for health, for the privilege of living in God's pure air and sunlight by holding up my head and walking erectly, joyously, as His child should. I am really insulting the Creator, to whom I pray, by reflecting such despair and degrading poverty in my mental attitude, thus erasing the divine image from my face. No matter how little I have, I can at least appear respectable. I can show that I respect myself by doing away as far as possible with the depressing appearance and influence of poverty."

Tidy up your little home and make it as neat and cheerful as possible. Do the same with your dress and general appearance. Keep yourself better groomed; look up, brace up, brush up, struggle up. Surround yourself with an atmosphere of hopefulness and show everybody by the new light in your eyes, the light of hope and expectancy of better things, that there is a change in you. Your neighbors will notice it. They will see a change in your home, in your wife, in your children. The change in the mental attitude of yourself and family, through facing toward the light instead of darkness, toward hope instead of despair, will make a tremendous change in your whole outlook on life.

In this way you are making yourself a prosperity magnet; you are radiating thought waves of hope, of ambition, of determination. Your new mental attitude is expressed in an erect, manly carriage, in squared, thrown back shoulders, in a neat, clean appearance, even though the clothing be old and threadbare, in a winning, forceful, magnetic countenance. You are thus establishing the conditions of success. The positive prosperity thought flows out like a wireless current and connects itself with similar thought currents. Hold the prosperity conviction, work steadily toward your object; see opportunity and success in your vista, determine to be somebody, hold firmly to the resolve, and your mentality will direct the invisible magnet of your personality to lift you higher and higher, to attract toward you others who will help you in the direction in which you are moving.

If you want a better position, more salary, money to pay off debts, or to get what you need, whatever it may be, cling with all the power of your mind to the thing you are trying to get, and never for a moment doubt you will get it. You do not inherit poverty, squalor. Lack and want have nothing whatever to do with God's children.

Your inheritance is divine, grand, sublime. Poverty is a mental disease, and you carry the antidote to its poison in your mind. You owe it to the One who has given you life, health, who has given you brains to make something of yourself, to improve your situation.

As long as you keep yourself saturated with the poverty conviction you cannot rise out of poverty. You must think yourself out of it. "The Lord is my Shepherd, and I cannot want." Hold that thought firmly and steadfastly in your mind. Believe it. Live up to it.

Abundance will never flow through pinched, doubting, poverty thoughts, any more than clear, crystal water can flow freely through foul, grease-clogged pipes. A right viewpoint must be your mental plumber to keep the connection open and free. Things of a kind attract one another. The poverty thought attracts more poverty, the fear thought more fear, the worry thought more worry, the anxiety thought more anxiety. On the other hand, the faith thought, trust thought, and the confidence thought attract things like themselves.

Poverty is a disease that can only be cured by prosperity remedies. The prosperity thought is the natural antidote for the poverty germ. It kills it. The poverty thought cannot exist in the mind at the same moment with the prosperity thought. One will drive out the other. It rests with you which one you will harbor and encourage.

Cling to the consciousness of your oneness with the All-Supply. Keep the supply pipes between you and the Infinite Source of all good always open. Don't pinch them. Don't cut off the supply by the limiting poverty thought, the doubt thought, the fear thought, the worry thought. Keep your supply pipes open by great faith in your Father-Mother-God, who is more solicitous for your welfare than any human parent could be. Hold fast to the anchor of your union with the Infinite Life; keep in the current running Godward and your life will not dry up or become barren, will not be blighted and blasted by the poverty drought.

The trouble with us is that we have been in the habit of looking for a material supply when our first supply must be mental. We keep the supply avenues open or we close them with our thoughts, our convictions. We materialize poverty by our doubting thoughts, by our fears of it. We are just beginning to find that we get out of this world what we think into it and work out of it, that our thought plan precedes its material realization just as the architect's plan precedes the building.

Remember that prosperity can not flow into your life while your mind is filled with poverty thoughts and convictions. We go in the direction of our thought and our convictions. By no law can you expect to get that which you do not believe you will get. Prosperity can not come to you if you are all the time driving it away from you by your poverty thought.

You must think in a positive determined way that you are going to succeed in whatever you desire to do or to be before you can expect success. That is the first condition by which you make yourself a magnet for the thing you are after. It doesn't matter whether it is work or money, a better position or health, or whatever else it is, your thoughts about it must be positive, clean cut, decisive, persistent. No weak, wobbly "Perhaps I may get it," or "Maybe it will come some time," or "I wonder if I shall get this," or "if I can do that" sort of thought will ever help you to get anything in this world or the next.

When young John Wanamaker started with a pushcart to deliver his first sale of clothing he turned on a positive current toward a merchant princeship. As he passed big clothing stores he pictured himself as a great merchant, owner of a much bigger establishment than any of those he saw, and he did not neutralize or weaken this thought current by all sorts of doubts or fears as to the possibility of reaching the goal of his ambition.

Most people think too much about blindly forcing themselves ahead. They do not realize that they can, by the power of thought, make themselves magnets to draw to them the things that will help them to get on. Wanamaker attracted to himself the forces that make a merchant prince. Every step he took was forward, to match the vision of his advance with its reality.

Marshall Field projected himself mentally out of a little country store into a clerkship in Chicago. Then he thought and worked himself out of this clerkship into a partnership. Still thinking and climbing upward, he next visualized himself at the head of the greatest merchandizing establishment in America, if not in the world. His mind always ran ahead. He was always picturing himself a little higher up, a little further on, always visualizing a larger business, and so making himself a magnet for the things he sought.

If John Wanamaker had been satisfied with himself at the start he would have remained in his first little store in Philadelphia, and thus cut off all possibility of becoming what he is—one of the greatest merchants the world has ever seen. If Marshall Field had stopped thinking himself higher up when the man he worked for in the little Pittsfield store predicted that he never would succeed as a merchant, he never would have been heard from. But Deacon Davis's telling Marshall Field's father that the boy would not make a salesman in a thousand years did not stop him thinking himself ahead. "On to Chicago, the City of Opportunity," he said to himself, and on and up he went until the little country merchant who predicted his failure was a Lilliputian in comparison.

The story of each of these men is, so far as the success principle is concerned, the story of every man who has ever succeeded in his undertakings. They may not have been conscious of the law underlying their methods, but they worked in unison with it, and hence succeeded.

The same thing is true of Andrew Carnegie, and of all the millionaires and self-made men among us who have raised themselves from poor boys to the ownership of colossal fortunes, or to commanding positions in some phase of the world's activities.

Any one who makes the accumulation of a fortune his chief goal, and who has grit, determination, will power and sufficient faith in himself to stick to his purpose will get there. But long before the youth who chooses such a goal has reached it, he will have dwarfed his manhood, and shriveled his soul.

To get away from poverty is one thing; to set one's heart on money as the ultimate good is another, and quite a different, thing. There is a whole world of difference between so saturating one's mind with the thought of money and its acquisition that there is no room for any other aspiration, and the constant dwelling on the black and hopeless poverty thought, the incessant picturing yourself as a pauper until you are so convinced of poverty's hold on you that you destroy the very ability which should help you to get away from it.

People who are down and out financially are down and out mentally. They are suffering from a mental disease of discouragement and loss of hope. There ought to be institutions conducted by government experts for the treatment of these poverty sufferers, for they are just as much in need of it as are the inmates of our hospitals. They need advice from mental experts. They have lost their way on the life path, and need to be shown the way back. They need to be turned about mentally, so that they will face the light instead of the darkness. They should be shown that they are stopping up their prosperity pipes, cutting off their source of supply by their pinching, poverty-stricken, limiting thought. Their whole mental attitude points toward failure, toward poverty, and by a natural law their outward conditions conform with the pictures they hold in mind.

This poverty disease could be cured in the case of the majority of down and outs, the failures, by proper mental treatments. If the people in the great failure army to-day could be shown that as long as they hold the poverty thought and go about with a sad, dejected expression on their faces, as though there were no hope in life for them, they will continue to be poor; but that if they will only turn about and face the sun, so that their shadows will fall behind them, their conditions will begin to improve, they would quickly take a new lease of life and courage. These mental prosperity treatments would generate in them a new hope that would cause them to brace up all along the line.

What a revelation would come to the poor people of the world if they would only eliminate from their minds for a single year the poverty thought; if they would erase from their minds poverty pictures and all the suggestions of grinding want that sadden and discourage; if, instead of expecting poverty, and all that the idea implies, they could go through one year expecting just the opposite,—prosperity,—visualizing, talking prosperity, thinking prosperity, acting as though they expected to be, as though they were, prosperous! Just this radical change of thought, this transposition of mental attitude, the persistent holding of the prosperous viewpoint for a year would not only change their whole outlook on life, but would revolutionize their material conditions.

They would brush up and clean up the things they have; their ambition would grow; their new way of looking at life would give an upward tendency to their surroundings. No matter how poor, their squalid aspect would go. Everything would take on a different appearance. There would be a new light in the people's faces. There would be hope there instead of despair,—expectancy of better things would give a glow of cheerfulness to their countenances. There would be a light in their eyes which never was there before. Working in the spirit of hope and expectancy of better things instead of that of discouragement and the fears of even greater poverty, they would forge ahead in a way that would astonish themselves.

The time is not far away when we shall have prosperity practitioners who will make a specialty of teaching people how to free their minds from thoughts that produce poverty by replacing them with their opposites, thus constantly enlarging the mental power of attraction until the mind becomes a powerful magnet, ever attracting prosperity.

These specialists will teach people the creative power of right thinking, and will show them how to attract their desires instead of killing them, as so many do, by wrong thinking. Clergymen of the future will do much toward eliminating poverty from among their people by instructing them to turn their backs on it and to face toward prosperity. They will teach them how to draw to themselves the sunlight of prosperity.

The cure of physical disease is effected by arousing the curative, restorative forces within the individual. These are brought into operation largely through faith in the physician, in the remedy, in the healer. The healthful mental attitude thus created overcomes the disease.

The cure of poverty,—poverty is usually a mental disease,—is effected in a similar way. The sufferer must first of all have faith in the great Physician of the universe. When that is fully and firmly established there will be no difficulty in flooding his mind with the prosperity thought, the thought that our Father-Mother-God is the Author of abundance, the Author of all the wealth of the earth, and that He is infinitely kinder and more solicitous for our welfare than the fondest mother could be for her child.

We have not yet tapped the possibilities of any part of the world's resources. Every inhabitant of the earth to-day is treading on secrets which would emancipate man from drudgery and allow him to live happily instead of merely to eke out a wretched subsistence as he has done up to the present. Hitherto, in the great majority of cases, we have barely been existing on the husks of things. Now we are beginning to taste the kernel, because we are coming into a knowledge of the powers locked up within ourselves, and also of the illimitable supply of God's abundance. Here and there, people are mastering the law of opulence. They are demonstrating that they can conquer poverty by making themselves prosperity magnets; that is, by thinking and working in conformity with the law of opulence, of abundance.

It is monstrous that so many of God's children are starving right on the shores past which the stream of inexhaustible plenty flows, a stream laden with all the rich things of the universe. There is no excuse for the horrible misery and suffering that exist in our midst. There is no reason why the children of the King of kings should be harassed and tortured, driven into premature graves by poverty, for the Creator has produced enough to make every one of His children rich, to give them an abundance of all they need. There is no necessity for those who have inherited all the good things of the earth to remain poor.

The very structure of the human machine indicates that it was intended for the best, that it was planned for comforts, for luxuries, and not for poverty-stricken conditions. If we could only realize the far-reaching influence of always expecting the best to come to us, always expecting opulence, success, we would never allow ourselves to be dominated by the black pictures of poverty and failure. If every one who is suffering from the limitations and humiliations imposed by a grinding poverty would proceed to establish the prosperity habit along the lines suggested; if they would, by continually holding the prosperous thought, convince the sub-conscious self that we were made to be successful, that prosperity belongs to us we should soon sight the millennium.

When we affirm our divinity, and claim our heritage; when we realize that our birthright keeps us in touch with the very Source of all supply, when we know that it was never intended that God's children should be poor or go hungry, that it was never intended they should live in poverty-stricken conditions, then we shall have struck the very basic principle of prosperity.

Hold the victorious attitude toward life and you will overcome all unfavorable conditions.

CHAPTER VIII

THE SUGGESTION OF INFERIORITY

As the initials which boys cut in the bark of a sapling become great, ugly scars on the grown tree, so the suggestions of inferiority etched upon the young mind become great ugly scars in the life of the adult.

You may succeed when others do not believe in you, when everybody else denounces you even, but never when you do not believe in yourself.

In olden times criminals, fugitives from justice, and slaves were branded. The words, "I am a fugitive," "I am a thief," or others indicating their crime or their inferior status were seared on some part of the body with a red hot iron.

In Rome robbers were branded on the forehead with a degrading letter. Laborers in mines, convicts, and gladiators were also branded. In Greece slaves were sometimes branded with a favorite poetical passage of their master. In France the branding iron used on slaves and criminals often took the form of the fleur-de-lis. In England desert ers from the army were marked with the letter D, and vagabonds, robbers and brawlers were branded in some way to advertise their disgrace.

The barbarous custom of branding human beings with the badge of crime or inferiority persisted in America even after it had been discontinued in the mother country. Hawthorne's "The Scarlet Letter" gives us a vivid picture of the suffering inflicted on the moral delinquent by Puritan moralists in Colonial days. The tragic heroine, Hester Prynn, is never allowed to forget her sin. The sinister scarlet letter with which she is branded proclaims her shame to every one she meets. While long after the Colonial period, up to the time of their emancipation, slaves were branded in Christian America with the initials of their owners as they were in Pagan Greece and Rome.

The mere idea of this stamping human beings with an indelible badge of disgrace, of inferiority, shocks us moderns. Yet we do not hesitate to mark people to-day with the scarlet letter of outlawry, the brand of ostracism. We put the criminal badge on our prisoners by shaving their heads and clothing them in stripes, thus perpetually keeping before them the suggestion that they are criminals, outlaws, apart from their kind.

We even carry our branding into our homes. In order to satisfy our cheap vanity, we force our domestic workers to wear as a mark of inferiority, a distinctive livery to remind them that they are menials, a lower grade of being than ourselves. As a matter of fact, if it were not for these branding distinctions, the maid would, in many instances, be taken for the mistress and the valet for the master whom they far outrank both in appearance and character.

There are certain inalienable rights which human beings inherit from their Maker, rights which no fellow being, no human law or authority is justified in taking away. No matter what offense a person may commit against society we have no right to degrade him below the level of a human being; we have no right so to bombard him with the suggestion of degradation, of inferiority, that we are almost certain to make him less a man; to lower his estimate of himself to such a degree that we rob him of the power even to attempt to regain his self-respect and his position in society. We have no right to insist that those who work for us shall wear a badge of inferiority. We have no right to thrust the suggestion of inferiority perpetually into the mind of any human being.

One of the greatest injuries we can inflict on any one is to convince him that he is a nobody, that he has no possibilities, and will never amount to anything. The suggestion of inferiority is responsible for more blighted ambitions, more stunted lives, more failures, more misery and unhappiness than almost any other single cause. Just as the constant dripping of water will wear away stone, so the constant iteration of a statement will cause its acceptance by the average person. Even though the facts may be opposed to it, a constant suggestion presented to the mind impresses us in spite of ourselves and tends to a conviction of its truth.

When the weight of the Civil War was nearly crushing Lincoln, when it was the fashion to denounce and criticise and condemn him, when he was being caricatured as a hideous monster in the jingo press all over the world, one day, walking the floor in the White House, he was overheard saying to himself, "Abe Lincoln, are you a dog or are you a man?" During these dark days it would appear that Lincoln sometimes had a doubt as to whether he was really the man his closest friends knew him to be, or the one an antagonistic press pictured him.

The curse of the inferiority suggestion not only tends to destroy our faith in ourselves, but it often makes even the innocent take on the appearance of guilt. When Lieutenant Dreyfus, through a foul conspiracy, was convicted of the crime of treason against France, he showed outwardly all the manifestations of guilt. When stripped, in the presence of a vast multitude, in a public square in Paris, of all his insignia of rank as an officer in the army of France, the epaulettes and buttons being cut from his uniform and his sword broken, although conscious of his innocence of the crime imputed to him he actually looked like the guilty thing he was accused of being. And all but a very few close friends in the vast concourse that witnessed his public disgrace believed that even his appearance corroborated his guilt. The brain of the unfortunate Dreyfus was a wireless receiving station for the hatred, the contempt of millions of people who believed they were looking at a vile traitor who had sold valuable military secrets to Germany.

We are all influenced for good or ill by suggestion, but children and young people are peculiarly susceptible to it. The constant suggestion of stupidity, badness, and dullness by teachers or parents, filling a child's mind with the idea that he is a blockhead, always blundering, making mistakes, that he is no good, and never will amount to anything, makes an indelible impression on his plastic mind.

The child naturally looks up to its parents and teachers and accepts what they say as truth. He has implicit faith in their superior knowledge and experience, which seem wonderful to him, and when they tell him he is stupid, dull, slow, or bad, he takes what they say for granted. He makes up his mind that, since they say so, he must be a blockhead, and that they are right in thinking he is no good and will never amount to anything.

It is criminal for a parent or teacher to brand a child as dull, stupid, bad; to tell him that there is nothing in him and that he will never be anybody or amount to anything in life. The effect on a sensitive child is disastrous. Thousands of boys and girls have been stunted mentally, their careers handicapped, and in some instances completely ruined by such cruel suggestions of inferiority.

I have known men who kept taunting their sons with what they called their imbecility and stupidity until the lads came to believe that they were partial idiots and could not possibly make anything of themselves. Many of them never did, because they were unable to overcome the conviction of inferiority impressed upon them by their fathers.

I remember one quite pathetic instance of a sensitive boy whose slightest mistake evoked a volley of abuse from his father. He would tell him that he was not "half baked," that he was "an imbecile," "a blockhead," "a blunderer," "a hopeless good-for-nothing." The little fellow so completely lost faith in himself and became so cowed that he hardly dared look people in the face. He could not be induced to enter his home when there were callers or guests present. He would slink away and hide himself in the shed or barn until they had gone. In fact, he became so morbid that he shrank from association even with other boys and the neighbors whom he had known from babyhood. The boy really had a fine mind, and when the death of his father threw him on his own resources, he managed, by sheer will force and dogged persistence, to succeed in making an honorable place in life. But he has never been able to get away from the early conviction of his inferiority, of his lack of ability compared with others around him. All his later life has been handicapped by those pernicious suggestions. Whenever he is asked to assume any responsibility, to take a place on a committee or a board, to speak in public or make himself prominent in any way, these boyhood mental pictures of his "good-for-nothingness" rise before him like terrifying ghosts and seriously cripple or paralyze his efforts. He has always felt that there is some grave defect in his nature and that, try as he may, he can not entirely overcome his handicap. This crippling, cramping defective image of himself impressed on this man in childhood and youth has robbed him of much of the best of life, of all the joy and exhilaration that come from spontaneity, from the free, unshackled expression of oneself, of all one's faculties.

Children are affected by praise or blame just as animals are. It is easy to kill the spirit of a dog by abuse and ill treatment, so that in a short time he will slink about with his tail between his legs, look guilty and self-depreciatory. In short, he will take on all the appearance of a "whipped cur." Thoroughbred horse trainers say that after a horse has been beaten or abused a few times he loses confidence in himself. His spirit is broken and when he sees the other horses getting neck and neck with him, or perhaps gaining on him a little, he is likely to give up the race. The destruction of self-confidence has caused many a youth with the latent qualities of a thoroughbred to fail in life's great race.

There are thousands and thousands of boys who do not develop quickly. Their brains are strong and capable, but they work slowly, and as a consequence the boys are misjudged and misunderstood by parents and teachers alike. In other instances the stupidity and dullness for which children are berated are only apparent. They are often the result of timidity, shyness, excessive self-consciousness. The youngsters do not dare to assert themselves. Especially is this true in families where the parental rule is stern and repressive. The children are afraid to speak aloud or to express themselves in any way.

74

The suggestion of inferiority deepens this defect till it becomes a mania. Many of the tragedies of the pernicious "ranking system" by examinations in our public schools and colleges are the result of an acute sense of inferiority. Every year quite a number of public school pupils and students in academies and colleges suffer nervous breakdown, become insane or commit suicide because they fail to pass their examinations. Chagrin and humiliation at the sense of inferiority suggested by their failure unbalances them. In most of those cases lack of confidence, not lack of ability, is the cause of failure.

You may say this is foolishness, but it is true. And if the suggestion of inferiority is powerful enough to drive young people to suicide, certainly the opposite, the suggestion of superiority, would multiply the youth's ability and work a miracle in his career.

A child should never hear the slightest hint to the effect that it is in any way inferior. Its whole training should tend to develop faith, confidence in himself, in his powers, in his great possibilities. As the twig is bent the tree is inclined. The child who is impressed in its tender formative stage with the idea of its inferiority suffers a wrong for which nothing in the after years can compensate.

Many young employees, especially if they are at all sensitive, are irreparably injured by nagging, fault-finding employers, who are constantly reminding them of their shortcomings, scolding them for every trivial mistake, and never giving them a word of praise or encouragement, no matter how creditable their work, or how well they deserve it.

Enthusiasm is the very soul of success and one cannot be enthusiastic about his work, he cannot take continued pride in it, if he is constantly being told that it is no good, that it is in fact disgracefully bad, that he should be ashamed of himself, and that he ought to quit if he can't do better. This fault-finding and continual suggestion of inferiority has ruined many a life.

A young writer, for instance, often gets a serious setback in his early efforts because of a severe criticism, an unqualified condemnation of his first book by a reviewer, or the return of his initial manuscript, with an editor's sneering suggestion that he has made a mistake in his calling. Harsh critics, editors and book reviewers have deterred many young writers from developing their talent. The fear of further criticism or humiliation, of being called foolish, dull or stupid, has blighted in the bud the career of many talented young people who under encouragement might have done splendid work. If he is of a sensitive nature even though he really have great ability such rebuffs often so dishearten him that he never has the confidence to try again.

In the same way many a possible clergyman or orator has been discouraged by early failure and the humiliation of ridicule. In other words, unless a youth is made of very strong material and has a lot of pluck and indomitable grit, the suggestion of inferiority, perpetual nagging and discouragement may seriously mar his career.

If instead of carping and harping on the little faults and mistakes of those under their jurisdiction, and prophesying their utter failure and ruin, parents, teachers, employers and others in responsible positions would recognize and appreciate laudable qualities, there would be less misery and crime in the world, fewer human failures and wrecks.

The perpetual suggestion of inferiority holds more people back from doing what they are capable of than almost anything else. In the Old World,—China, Japan, India, in England and other European countries, for example,—who can measure the harm it has done in the form of "caste." Think what superb men and women have been held down all their lives, kept in menial positions, because they were reared in the belief that once a servant always a servant; that because their parents were menials they must also be menials!

What splendid brains and fine personalities we see serving in hotels, restaurants and private households in Europe—often much superior to the proprietors themselves. Saturated with the idea that the son must follow in the father's footsteps, though they may be infinitely superior in natural ability to those they serve, these men remain waiters, butlers, coachmen, gardeners or humble employees of some sort. No matter what talents they possess they are held in leash by the ingrained conviction of generations that the accident of birth has decided their position in life. They are convinced that the barriers established by heredity and by caste, an outworn feudal system, are insurmountable.

How delightfully the gentle humorist Barrie satirizes this Old World condition in his play, "The Admirable Crichton." How skillfully he portrays the clever and resourceful butler, Crichton, who in the crucible of a great emergency proves himself a born leader, a man head and shoulders above the noble lord, his master.

When the yacht carrying the master and his family, Crichton and some other servants, is wrecked, they escape with their lives to a desert island. In their desperate plight the barriers of caste are broken down, and master and man change places. Removed from an artificial environment, where hereditary rank and wealth determine the status of the man, Nature unmistakably asserts herself, and Crichton, by the tacit consent of all, becomes leader. By the force of his inborn ability he controls the situation. He commands, the others obey. Yet when they are rescued by a passing ship and brought back to England, old conditions at once resume their sway. Crichton, without a murmur, or thought of change, falls back to his former menial position, and all goes on as before.

While we Americans laugh at, or severely criticize and denounce, the snobbishness of class distinctions in other countries, we are guilty of similar snobbishness, especially in regard to one section of our fellow-Americans—the Negro race. No matter how highly educated, how able, how refined or charming a man or a woman, if he or she has but a drop of Negro blood, we brand him or her with the stigma of race inferiority.

I always feel sympathy for the colored people, especially for the better educated and more refined men and women of this class who must suffer keenly from the discrimination against their race. They see white people avoiding them everywhere; refusing to sit down beside them in public places, in churches, on trains and cars, everywhere they can possibly avoid it. In the South they are not permitted to ride in the same cars with whites, and in other parts of the country, while they may travel on the ordinary day coaches, they are not allowed on the Pullman cars, except as waiters and porters. Our hotels, private schools, public places, and even many of our churches, practice similar discrimination. The churches pretend to draw no color lines, but by their attitude most of them practically do so.

Everywhere they turn in this land of ours, where we boast that every man is "born free and equal," Negroes are embarrassed, placed at a disadvantage. In all sorts of ways white people are constantly humiliating them, reminding them that they belong to an inferior race, and they take their places according to the valuation of those born to more favorable conditions. This constant suggestion of inferiority has done much to keep the colored race back, because it has added tremendously to their sense of real or fancied inferiority and has been a discouragement to their efforts to make themselves the equals of those who look down upon them.

We can not help being influenced by other people's opinion of us. It makes us, according to its nature, think more or less of ourselves, of our ability. We are similarly affected by our environment. We unconsciously take on the superiority or inferiority of our surroundings. Employees who work in cheap, shoddy stores or factories soon become tagged all over with the marks of inferiority, the cheap John methods employed in the establishments in which they work and spend their days.

If the employees in a store like Tiffany's or Altman's, for example, were to be mixed up with those of some of the cheap, shoddy New York stores, it would not take much discernment to pick out the worker in the superior environment from the one in the inferior. To spend one's best years selling cheap, shoddy merchandise will inevitably leave its mark on those who do so. Even though we may struggle against it, we are unconsciously dyed by the quality of our occupation, the character of the concerns for which we work.

In making your life choice, avoid as you would poison shoddy, fakey concerns which have no standing in their community. Keep away from occupations that have a demoralizing tendency. Every suggestion of inferiority is contagious, and helps to swerve the life from its possibilities.

Every influence in our environment is a suggestion which becomes a part of us. If we live with people who lack ambition, who are slovenly, slipshod, or with people of loose morals, of low flying ideals, we tend to reflect their qualities. If we mingle much with those who use slangy, vulgar, incorrect English, people who are not careful about their manners or their expression, these things will reappear in our own conversation and manners. If we read inferior books, or associate with perpetual failures, with people who botch their work and botch their lives our own standards will suffer from the contagion.

It does not matter whether inferiority relates to manner, to work, to conversation, to companions, to thought habits—wherever it occurs, its tendency is to pull down all standards and to cut down the average of achievement. We are all living sensitive plates on which the example, the thoughts and suggestions of others, our own thoughts and habits, our associations and surroundings indelibly etch themselves.

I wish I could burn it into the consciousness of every person who wants to make a success of life that he cannot do so while he associates himself with inferiority and harbors a low estimate of himself. Get away from both. Have nothing to do with them. If you are a victim of the inferiority suggestion, deny the suggestion, drive it from your mind as the greatest enemy of your welfare.

You can only do what you think you can. If you hold in mind a cheap, discreditable picture of yourself; if you doubt your efficiency you are shackled, you are not free to express yourself. You erect a barrier between yourself and the power that achieves.

The mere mental acknowledgment or feeling that you are weak, inefficient, is contagious. It is sensed by other people and their thought is added to yours in undermining your self-confidence, which is the bulwark of achievement. No matter what others say or think of you, always hold in mind a lofty ideal of yourself, a picture of your own efficiency. Never allow yourself to doubt your ability to do what you undertake. You can not be inferior, because you are made in God's image. You can, if you will, make a masterpiece of your life, because it is part of His plan that you should.

CHAPTER IX

HAVE YOU TRIED LOVE'S WAY?

Love, like the sun, never sees the dark side of anything.
You can purchase a man's labor, you've got to cultivate his good will.
Sweeter than the perfume of roses is the possession of a kind, charitable, unselfish nature, a ready disposition to do for others any good turn in one's power.

A New York man who saw a little girl carrying a crippled boy across a street, offered to assist her, telling her that the boy was too heavy for her to carry. "Oh, no," said the child quickly, "he's not heavy; he's my brother."

Oh, marvelous power of love that lightens all heavy burdens and smooths all rough roads! What would become of humanity were it not for love, which sweetens the hardest labor and makes self-sacrifice a joy? It is the greatest force in the universe. Without its transform ing power we should still be primitive barbarians.

In spite of the loud cries of pessimists and skeptics to the contrary, its light is still leading men upward. Although the dream of the world's peacemakers has come to naught and Europe is plunged in a merciless war, yet there are multitudes of signs of the reign of love. Its merciful healing power is at work even on the cruel battlefield. We see it animating the great army of Red Cross surgeons and nurses, who, regardless of creed or country, racial or social differences, are treating all the wounded soldiers as brothers, binding up their wounds and nursing them back to health and life. Love is healing the hurts made by hate and discord.

We see its influence in the miracle which the leaven of the Golden Rule is performing in the business world, in the passion for social service in the world at large, in the gradual obliteration of class distinctions, in the growing efforts to ameliorate the conditions of the poor, in the great wave of reform that is beating against the walls of all our institutions, our jails, our poorhouses, our reformatories, our insane asylums. The abuses with which these places were filled are gradually being cleared up by love.

In many of our prisons, the kindly, brotherhood system of treatment that has been inaugurated is really helping to reform criminals, whereas the old system of penology killed men, broke their spirit, or made them more hardened in crime. It rarely, if ever, reformed. Love's way must in time banish altogether the old cruel prison methods, and ultimately the criminal himself. When the world is run by love, by the Golden Rule plan, crime will die a natural death.

Every one who slips from the right path, no matter what he has done, should be given another chance, a fresh opportunity to make good, to rebuild his character. One who has sinned against society should not be expelled from the sympathies, the good-will and the kindliness of his fellowmen. Criminals should be treated as unfortunate brothers and sisters who have stumbled and lost their way on the life path. Love is the only medium that will help them to rise, to get back into the current that runs Godward.

People who understand them, who see a God in the ruins that evil influences have made, would make good men and women out of the great majority of our prisoners.

Many of these poor wretches never had an opportunity. They never felt the magic touch of love, never knew the influence of a good home, of honest, loving parents. Most of them did not have a right start in life. They were handicapped at birth by ignorance, by disease, by vicious parentage. They never had a fair chance. Love's way would give them one. Shutting them into cramped, miserable, sunless cells, with none of the comforts or conveniences of life, where none of the humanities reach them; meting them out treatment we would not dream of inflicting on our domestic animals, is like trying to put out fire with kerosene oil. Such treatment makes them worse, arouses their basest passions of revenge, bitterness and hatred, fills them with a determination to "get even" with society.

Society is beginning to wake up to the futility of such brutal methods. It is beginning to apply love's way to its criminal classes, to all classes.

Our free hospitals, our homes for the aged and poor, our public asylums, are all, like our prisons, working upward toward the light. The fallen, the sick, the poor, the old, the maimed, the bruised and suffering, everywhere are receiving more consideration, more humane treatment, more kindness. And we are finding that greater trust in them, greater sympathy and greater interest in our unfortunate brothers and sisters, are working a marvelous change in human conditions.

In other words, in spite of many seeming contradictions, many glaring evils in our midst, many setbacks and discouragements, the spirit of the Christ, of the Golden Rule, is acting like a healing leaven and performing miracles in the great human mass.

Love is the great mind opener, the great heart opener and life-enricher, the great developer. It is what holds society together, and if children were trained to love humanity, to love all countries and their inhabitants as they are taught to love their own country and countrymen, there would be no wars. War proceeds largely from what is called patriotism. And patriotism in its narrower sense, which seeks only its own good, its own aggrandizement, at the expense of other countries and peoples, has ever been the curse of the race. When our love is big enough to say, "The world is my country," wars will cease.

A few days ago I was attracted by an advertisement in a morning paper which said, "When every other physician has given you up; when you have failed to find relief from all other sources, then come to me. You are the sort of person I cure." The advertiser may have been a quack, but the advertisement would make its appeal, perhaps, to the desperate, the discouraged, who had been given up as incurable by the regular profession, and it set me to thinking. "Why, this," I said to myself, "is the language of Divine Love's advertisement. 'Come unto me all ye that labor and are heavy laden and I will give you rest.' When you have failed to find comfort, satisfaction or joy in anything else, when your friends have deserted you, when your business is ruined, when you have made fatal mistakes and society has closed its doors on you, when everybody else rejects and denounces you, when everything else has failed, then come to me and you shall find peace and rest."

Love is the sovereign remedy. It is the last resort of those driven to desperation. When nothing else is left, when life is full of bitterness and anguish, the thief, the murderer, the failure, the outcast turns to Love and finds a refuge, for "Love never faileth."

Love is to every human being what mother love is to the erring child. No son or daughter has ever fallen so low as to get beyond a mother's love. When society has turned its back on the outcast, when the prison door closes behind him, when companions have fled, when sympathy and mercy have departed, when the world has forgotten, the mother remembers and loves her child. She visits her boy in the "death house," her daughter in the dens of vice in the slums. The child can never stray too far for the mother's love to follow. It is the most perfect prototype of our Father-Mother-God's love.

The Vedanta scriptures, which are thousands of years older than the Old Testament of our Bible, commanded us to love our neighbors as ourselves because we are all neighbors, because of the oneness of all life, because the same spirit is in all human beings. Until we see and live in conscious coöperation with this oneness of spirit, until the world sees it in all human beings, there will be public strife, private quarrels, greed, selfish ambition, inhumanity of man to man, poverty, crime, all sorts of wretchedness and misery. Love alone can wipe all these out. Human laws, repression, punishment will never do it. Christ's way, Love's way, holds the solution of all life's problems.

I was talking recently with a cold-blooded, overbearing, brow-beating business man who told me he was going out of business because he was so tired and sick of incompetent, dishonest help. His employees, he said, were always taking advantage of him, stealing, spoiling merchandise, blundering, shirking, clipping their hours. They took no interest in his welfare, their only concern being in what they found in their pay envelope. "I have enough to live on," he concluded, "and I don't propose to run a business for their benefit. I have tried every means I know of to get good work out of ignorant, selfish help, but it is no use, and now I have done with it. My nervous system is worn out and I must give up the game."

"You say you have tried everything you could think of in managing your employees, but has it ever occurred to you to try Love's way?" I asked.

"Love's way!" he said disgustedly. "What do you mean by that? Why, if I didn't use a club all the time my help would ride right over me and ruin me. For years I have had to employ detectives and spies to protect my interests. What do these people know about love? Why I would have the red flag out here in no time if I should attempt any such fool business as that."

A young man who had been successful in Golden Rule management hearing of the situation saw in it a possible opening, and asked this man to give him a trial as manager before giving up his business altogether.

The result was, he was so pleased with him that in less than half an hour he had engaged him as manager, although he still insisted that it was a very doubtful experiment.

The first thing the new man did on taking charge was to call the employees in each department together and have a heart to heart talk with them. He told them that he had come there not only as a friend of the proprietor, but as their friend also, and that he would do everything in his power to advance their interests as well as those of the business. The house, he told them, had been losing money for years, and it was up to him and them to change all that and put the

83

balance on the right side of the ledger. He made them see that harmony and coöperation are the basis of any real success for a concern and its employees.

From the start he was cheerful, hopeful, sympathetic, enthusiastic, encouraging. He quickly won the confidence and good will of everybody in the establishment, and had them all working as heartily for the success of the business as if it were their own. The place was like a great beehive, where all were industrious, happy, contented, working for the hive. So great was the change that customers began to talk about the new spirit in the house. Business grew and prospered, and in an incredibly short time, the concern was making instead of losing money.

Yet in many respects the new manager was not nearly as able as his employer, but he had a different spirit. He was animated by a belief in the brotherhood of man. He had sympathy, tact, diplomacy, and a real personal interest in those who worked under him. He never scolded them when they did not do right; he simply talked with them like an elder brother and made them ashamed of themselves. He showed them there was a better way, and they followed it. In short, he won their love and respect and they would do anything for him.

The Golden Rule method had driven out hate, selfishness, greed and dissension. The interests of all were centered on the general welfare, and so all prospered. When the proprietor returned from abroad, whither he had gone for a few months' rest and recuperation, he could scarcely believe in the reality of the transformation that "love's way" had effected in his old employees and in the entire establishment.

You who have been tortured and torn to pieces for years with hot tempers, with worry, with fear, with hatred and ill will; you who have already committed suicide on many years of your life, why not turn your back on all this and try love's way? So far your life has been a disappointment. There must be a better way for all who bear the scars and stains of strife, who have been battered and buffeted by the old evil way, in which there has been no rest, no harmony, no sweetness. Why not try love's way? Try it for every trouble, for every hurt and sorrow.

Try it you whose home life has been a bitter disappointment; you husbands and wives who have quarreled, who have never known what peace and comfort are, try love's way. It will smooth out all your wrinkles, it will put a new spirit into your home that was never there before, it will bring a new light into your eyes, new hope into your heart, and new joy into your life.

84

You mothers who have worn yourselves to a frazzle and prematurely aged yourselves in trying to bring up your children by scolding, nagging, punishing, driving, why not try love's way instead? You can love your boys and girls into obedience and respect much more quickly and with far better results to them and to yourself than by driving them; appeal to their best and noblest instincts instead of their worst, and you will be surprised how quickly and readily they will respond to your appeal. There is something in human nature which protests against being driven or forced. If you have been trying to force your boys and girls in the past, give it up and try the new way, love's way. See if it does not work wonders in your home. See if it will not make your domestic machinery run much more smoothly. See if it will not wonderfully relieve the strain upon yourself. Give love's way a trial.

Try it, you fault-finding, scolding housewife. Instead of nagging your family, fretting and stewing from morning till night, blaming, upbraiding, complaining, try love's way. Instead of berating a maid before your guests when she accidentally breaks a piece of china, put yourself in her place, try to realize her embarrassment, and pass over the mishap cheerfully. Then, in private, give her a gentle word of caution. She will be more careful in the future. If your laundress returns a piece of smirched linen, or if her work is not quite so well done as it was the last time, don't give her a brutal scolding. Harsh treatment will only make her sullen and unhappy, but you will find her susceptible to kindness and gentle words.

Give sympathy and kindness instead of scolding and nagging and you will work a revolution in your household. You will be delighted to find how quickly love's way will change the atmosphere in your family, how soon helpful relations will take the place of antagonistic ones. Praise, generous, whole-hearted, unstinted praise, now and then, will not hurt any one, but, on the contrary, will act like lubricating oil on dry squeaky machinery, and its reflex action on yourself will be magical.

You husbands who have been substituting money and luxury for love, who have thought that if a woman had a fine house, beautiful clothes and all her bills paid, she ought to be satisfied and happy; you who have so miserably failed of your object in this substitution will be surprised to find how much happier you can make your wife by bestowing on her a generous, unselfish love. A very little money, a very humble home with love will make every true woman happier than millions, a palatial home, with indifference.

Try love's way, you men who have been lording it over your families, bullying and brow-beating your wives and children, using slave-driving methods in your home. You know that this old brutal way has not brought you happiness or satisfaction; you have always been disappointed with it, then why not try the new philosophy, try love's way? It is the great cure-all, it is the Christ remedy which is leavening the world.

Try it you who are worn out with the discord and the hagglings, the trials and tribulations you encounter every day in your business. You men and women who have never been able to get good help, who are driven to desperation with the wicked breakage and wastage of your employees; you who have been through purgatory in your struggle with dishonesty and inefficiency, whose faces are furrowed with cruel wrinkles and prematurely aged in trying to fight evil with evil, try love's way. It will create a new spirit in your store, your factory, your office. Whatever your business, whatever your trials and difficulties, love will ease the jolts of life and smooth your way miraculously. Try love's way all you who have hitherto lived in purgatory because you did not know this better way.

You have tried the "getting square" policy, the hatred and grudge method; you have tried the revenge way, the jealousy way; you have tried the worry, the anxiety method, and these have pained and tortured you all the more. You have tried law and the courts to settle troubles and difficulties with neighbors and business associates, and perhaps you won lawsuits only to make bitter, life-long enemies. But perhaps you have never yet tried love's way, excepting in spots. If you have not yet tried it as a principle, as a life philosophy, as a great life lubricant, begin now. It will smooth out all the rough places and wonderfully ease your journey over the jolts of life.

You may be wondering why you have so few friends, why you do not attract people, why others are not more interested in you. Look into your heart and you will find the reason. If you are sending out a current of selfishness, of uncharitableness, unkindness, indifference, ingratitude, you can not get a return current of friendship, of encouragement and helpfulness. The stream that leads back to you will be just like that which goes out in your thought, in your habitual mental attitude. To have friends, to win love you must make yourself a magnet for love. You must send out the friendly thought current, the helpful current, the kindly, loving current of human fellowship. If you give out stinginess, narrowness, meanness, selfishness, you will not receive love's gifts in return. As you give, so will you receive, and the more generously you give of love and kindness and service the more generously will the current that returns bear them back to you.

The most beautiful thing on this earth, that which every human being craves most is love. It is, as Henry Ward Beecher said, "the river of life in this world. Think not that ye know it who stand at the little tinkling rill, the first small fountain. Not until you have gone through the rocky gorges, and not lost the stream; not until you have gone through the meadow, and the stream has widened and deepened until fleets could ride on its bosom; not until beyond the meadow you have come to the unfathomable ocean, and poured your treasures into its depths—not until then can you know what love is."

All through the Bible are passages which extol the height and depth, the breadth and power, the inexhaustibleness of love. The more of love we give out, the more we have. Love maintains perpetual summer in the soul and shuts out winter's chill. Love of man is love of God, and love of God prolongs life.

"With long life will I satisfy him," declares Jehovah in the words of the Psalmist, "because he hath set his love upon me." Love is harmony, and harmony prolongs life, as fear, jealousy, envy, friction, and discord shorten it. Those who are filled with the spirit of love, whose sympathies are not confined to their own family, but reach out to every member of the human family, are more exempt from the ills of mankind than the selfish and pessimistic, who lose the better part of life, the joy and the strength that come from giving themselves to others.

Some natures are so permeated with the spirit of love, of helpfulness, of unselfishness, that their very presence acts like a balm upon the wounded soul. They radiate harmony, soul sunshine. There is a personal charm about them which strengthens, reassures, and uplifts.

No more scientific advice was ever uttered on this earth than "Love your enemies." Nothing will take the sting out of unkindness like kindness; nothing will disarm prejudice, hatred, and jealousy like love. It is impossible for any one to continue to hate us, when we send out to him only love thoughts, love vibrations, or to be jealous of us when we send out to him only kindly, generous, helpful thoughts. Hatred or the spirit of revenge cannot live in the presence of love any more than an acid can retain its eating, biting qualities in the presence of an alkali.

One whose heart is filled with love for all cannot possibly have an enemy very long, because love dissolves all enmity, all jealousy, neutralizes, antidotes all hatred. One-sided hatred cannot exist because there is nothing to keep it alive. It must be fed in some way or the fire will die out for lack of fuel.

It is simply impossible to keep on feeling unkindly towards another, to continue hating him very long when we discover that he feels kindly toward us and is willing to help us. I have never felt so humiliated in my life as when years ago, in my hot youth, I was rendered a very great service by a man whom I disliked intensely, and against whom I had for some time cherished a grudge. His great-hearted, generous act, which was a real help to me, made me feel utterly ashamed of myself. It showed me as nothing else could have done what a mean, unworthy, contemptible thing it is to nurse a feeling of hate or revenge toward a fellow-being.

We cannot hold the love thought without feeling the uplift, the glow, the divine energy which it sends through the whole system. Nor, on the other hand, can we hold the hate thought, the revenge, the jealous, the envious, or any other mean, selfish thought, without a feeling of depression, a feeling of smallness, of contemptibleness, which robs us of self-respect and of power.

When you denounce and condemn others, when you nurse bitterness and ill will in your heart, you start boomerang vibrations which impair your cell life and seriously mar your happiness and efficiency. One of the great benefits of devotional exercise, of prayer, of contemplation, of divine thinking, is that this mental attitude sets in motion vibrations which have a helpful, uplifting influence on both mind and body. Where love and affection are habitually vibrating through the cell life they develop a poise and serenity of character, a sweetness and strength, a peace and satisfaction that reënforce the whole being. Love soothes and strengthens. Hate lacerates, wrinkles, weakens. The character of people who keep themselves continually stirred up by discordant emotions, who live in discordant homes where there is perpetual wrangling, criticism, denunciation, scolding, twitting are cold, skeptical, unlovely, selfish. Their affections become marbleized. There is nothing outside of vice which will deform the character so quickly as living in an atmosphere of perpetual hatred, jealousy, envy and revenge. The wear and tear of their vicious vibrations is ever getting in its deadly work.

Love is the great disciplinarian, the supreme harmonizer, the true peacemaker. It is the great balm for all that blights happiness or breeds discontent, a sovereign panacea for malice, revenge, and all brutish passions and propensities. As cruelty melts before kindness, so the evil passions find their antidote in sweet charity and loving sympathy.

One reason why a happy home is the sweetest, most beautiful spot on earth is because the love atmosphere, the harmony vibrations give a blessed sensation of harmony, of rest, of safety, security and power. The moment we enter such a place we feel its soothing, reassuring, uplifting atmosphere. It produces a feeling of mental poise, of serenity which we do not experience anywhere else.

During a recent visit to a large family I was much impressed by the power of one person to create this beautiful home spirit. In this family was one sister who, though the youngest member, seemed to take the place of the mother, who was dead. This young girl was the apparent center of the home. Nothing of importance was undertaken by any of her brothers without consulting her. Not one of them would leave the house without first kissing her good-by, and she was the first one they sought when they came home. They all seemed anxious to confide to her their little secrets, to tell her of what had happened to them during the day, to have her opinion and advice in all difficulties.

The secret of this young girl's influence lay in her great interest in the boys, and her wonderful love for them. In talking with the brothers I discovered that each thought that the sister was especially interested in him and his affairs, and that he would not think of undertaking or deciding anything of importance without first consulting her. Each and all of them seemed to prefer her company to that of any other young lady, and were always proud to escort her when she went anywhere. Those boys are all clean-minded, open, frank and chivalrous, and I could not help thinking that a great deal of it was due to the sister's influence.

"To love, and to be loved," said Sydney Smith, "is the greatest happiness of existence." Every one, rich and poor, high and low, is reaching out for love. What will not a man do to win the love of one who embodies his ideal of womanhood; one in whom he sees all the beautiful qualities that he himself lacks! This love is really a divine hunger, the longing for possession of what would make him a whole man instead of the half one he feels he is.

Why is it that when a coarse-grained, brutal, dissipated man falls in love with a sweet, pure girl he immediately changes his ways, looks up, thinks up, braces up, drops his profanity, is more refined, more choice in his language, more exclusive in his associations, and is, to all appearances, for the time at least, a changed man? Simply because love is a more powerful motive to the man than dissipation. He drops the latter, and if his love is steady and true he will never again indulge in any degrading practice.

Who has not seen the magic power of love in transforming rough, uncouth men into refined and devoted husbands? I have known women who had such great, loving, helpful hearts, and such charm of manner, that the worst men, the most hardened characters would do anything in the world for them—would give up their lives even to protect them. But these men could not be reformed by prison methods, could not be touched by unkindness or compulsion. Love is the only power that could reach them.

I do not believe there is any human being, in prison or out, so depraved, so low, so bad but that there is somebody in the world who could control him perfectly by love, by kindness, by patience. Many a man has been kept from performing a disgraceful, a criminal act by the thought that somebody loved him, believed in him, trusted him.

"Though thy sins be as scarlet they shall be made whiter than snow." Love purifies, lifts up, regenerates. We are all familiar with its wonderful transforming power; how it erases the scars of sin, smooths out the wrinkles which vice has left in the face, softens the hard features and puts its own divine stamp there. We know how it changes the coarse, brutal, sinful man into its own divine likeness, how it brings the color back to the pale cheek, the luster to the dull eye, how it restores courage to the disheartened, hope to the distressed and the despairing. We know how it calls into the face a light which was never there before, and which is not of earth.

In the remarkable play, "The Passing of the Third Floor Back," we have a striking illustration of the subtle, silent force of the love motive. Those who have seen or read the play will remember how in response to an advertisement in a London paper, "Room to let, Third floor back," comes a remarkable man, who is given the title of "The Stranger." This man takes the "third floor back," and finds himself in a boarding house filled with questionable characters, petty thieves, gamblers, people who have led fast lives, all sorts of uncharitable, envious men and women. They stoop to every kind of meanness. One woman even steals candles. Every one tries to cheat every one else and is cheated in return. The landlady is of the same type as her boarders. She preys on them and they prey on her. She waters the milk and adulterates the food. Then to keep herself from being robbed she puts everything under lock and key.

The mere presence of the Stranger seems antagonistic to the practices and low-flying ideals of the boarders and the landlady. They begin to make all sorts of fun of him. But he takes no notice. Instead he gives them kindness for unkindness, love for hate, and a pleasant smile as the only answer to their sarcastic, cutting remarks and innuendoes. Gradually, as they become better acquainted, he begins to talk to them of themselves, to point out their good qualities, and to show them what great ability they have in certain lines, what wonderful things are possible to them.

He told one of the young men who had made merry at his

expense that he had a fine artistic temperament, and that he had in him the making of a great artist. He showed another his possibilities as a musician, and so on with every member of the discordant, jangling group, until each one finally came under the spell of his love and kindness.

The little London "slavey," or maid-of-all-work who was abused and constantly reminded that she had been in State Prison and hence was a nobody, under the Stranger's uplifting influence became a self-respecting, noble woman. The landlady, who had hitherto treated the girl like a slave, began to favor her and made her go outdoors and get a little change while she did the work. A man and wife who had lived a cat and dog life were brought together in harmony. All of the boarders, without exception, even those who had been the most brutal and selfish, gradually changed and became thoughtful, helpful and kindly toward one another. They became friends. The whole atmosphere of the house was changed. The Stranger had shown every man and woman of them his or her better self, and in so doing had literally made them anew.

Thus did one who typified the Christ spirit, a simple, quiet man who loved his fellowmen and who found his greatest joy in serving others, manage to divert all of these people out of the crooked channels in which they had lived and into the right path toward happiness. Love, discovering to them these higher possible selves, transformed them. This is love's way.

Love tames the fiercest animals. How quickly their wild, ferocious expression is replaced by a milder, softer, more gentle one under the kindly treatment of one who really loves them, one who looks upon them as did St. Francis, as his "little dumb brothers and sisters." The brute nature is gradually softened and distrust gives way to confidence. The suspicious look is replaced by a trustful one. Affection takes the place of dislike and fear; love goes out to meet love. Is there any more beautiful illustration in Nature of the influence of love and kindly treatment than the evolution of our pet dogs from the ferocious wolf? Note the gentle, peaceful face of a cow or a horse which has been brought up as a family pet. Such animals would not step on or injure a child any more than we would ourselves. We love and trust them and they love and trust us in return. Love begets love.

Some people mistake selfishness or self-love for real love. Everywhere we see the sort of base substitute which says, "If you do this for me I'll do that for you." The woman that says to a man, in her heart, if not with her lips, "If you'll support me and give me a home, I'll love you," does not love. This is selfishness. A great many people confuse love of the thing given with love of the giver. They mistake the love of their own comforts, of a good time, of dress and luxuries, for love of the person who supplies them with these things. This is a mere travesty of the genuine thing. Love simply loves and asks nothing in return. There is no self in it. Abuse, bitterness, indifference, ingratitude do not change or destroy love. It simply loves on. And no love is ever lost, whether it is returned or not. Genuine love is a force that always wins out. Even if it is not reciprocated it wins by chastening, softening, elevating, beautifying and enriching the life of the one who loves. This is love's way.

What mothers endure for many years for their children would kill them or drive them to an insane asylum in half the time but for love. This is the healing balm that cures all hurts, lightens all burdens, that takes the drudgery out of service. It is love alone that enables the poor mother to risk her life for her child, to go through terrible experiences in her struggles with poverty and sickness to rear her children. A burden half as great which had no love in it would crush the life out of her. But love lightens the load, takes the sting out of poverty, the pain out of sacrifice.

The same thing is true of the loving father, though his burden in the nature of things is rarely as heavy as the mother's. But he is often virtually a slave for half a lifetime or more for those he loves, and if he is a real man he does not complain. Love lightens the burden and cheers the way. Where the heart is, there the burden is light.

"A new commandment give I unto you, that ye love one another; as I have loved you love ye also one another."

In the literal fulfilling of this commandment lies the salvation of the world. Among the many noble souls of our own time who have tried to live in accordance with it, one of the most conspicuous was Count Leo Tolstoy. In one of his own beautiful stories Tolstoy shows how every one, no matter what his station or how poor his circumstances, may do this, by following the Master's example in treating every human being as we would a loved member of our own family.

A very devout Russian peasant, so runs the story, had prayed for years that the Master might sometime come to his humble cabin home. One night he had a vision in which the Master appeared to him, and told him He would come to his cabin next day.

Filled with joy, the peasant awoke. So real seemed his vision that he arose and immediately went to work putting his cabin to rights and preparing for the expected heavenly guest.

A terrible storm of sleet and snow raged throughout the day.

While performing his simple household duties, heaping fresh logs in his crude fireplace, preparing his pot of cabbage soup, the Russian peasant's daily dish, the man would look out into the storm with anxious, expectant eyes. Presently he saw a poor half-frozen peddler with a pack on his back struggling toward the light, but almost overcome by the fierce blasts of snow and sleet that beat upon him. The peasant rushed out and brought the wayfarer into his cabin. He dried his clothing, warmed him, fed him some of the cabbage soup, and started him on his way again, comforted and rejoicing.

In a little while he saw another traveler, a poor old woman, trying feebly to beat her way against the blinding snow. Her also the compassionate peasant took into his cabin. He warmed and fed her, wrapped his own coat about her, and, strengthened and encouraged, sent her too on her way.

The day wore slowly away and darkness approached, but still no sign of the Master. Hoping against hope, the man went once again to his cabin door, and looking out into the storm he saw a little child, who was utterly unable to make its way against the blinding sleet and ice. He took the half-frozen child in his arms, brought it into the cabin, warmed and fed it, and soon the little wanderer fell asleep before the fire.

Sorely disappointed because the Master had not appeared, the peasant sat gazing into the fire, and as he gazed he fell asleep. Suddenly the room was radiant with a light that did not come from the fire, and there stood the Master, white-robed, and serene, looking upon him with a smile. "Ah, Master, I have waited and watched all this long day, but thou didst not come." The Master replied, "Three times have I visited thy cabin to-day. The poor peddler whom thou rescued, warmed and fed, that was I; the poor woman to whom thou gavest thy coat, that was I; and this little child whom thou hast saved from the tempest, that is I. Inasmuch as ye have done it unto the least of these, you have done it unto me."

The Christ vision faded. The peasant awoke. He was alone with the child, who was smiling in its sleep. But he knew that the Master had visited his cabin.

> *"The love of God! The love of God!" I said,—*
> *And at the words through all my being went*
> *A sudden shudder of light; the firmament*
> *Not otherwise seems riven by the red*
> *Jagg'd lightning-flash that quivers overhead*
> *When for an instant heaven and earth are blent,*
> *So for a dazzling space my heart was rent,*

And I beheld—beheld—but all had fled.
Had fled! nor has returned; yet on my way
Along the pave or through the clanging mart,
Sometimes a stranger's eye falls full on mine;
"You too?" We have no speech, we make no sign,
But something seems to pass from heart to heart,
And I am full of gladness all that day.

C. A. Price in Scribner's Magazine.

CHAPTER X

WHERE YOUR SUPPLY IS

He who dares assert the I,
May calmly wait
While hurrying fate
Meets his demand with sure supply.

Helen Wilmans.

Never affirm, or think about yourself, your prospects, your career, or your happiness what you do not wish to come true.
Every child should be taught to expect success and happiness, to believe that the good things of the world are intended for him.
We never can get more out of ourselves than we expect. If we expect large things, demand them; if we hold the large mental attitude toward our work, toward life, we shall get much greater results than if we depreciate ourselves, and look for only little things.

That man who dares not "assert the I" with undaunted assurance, with the conscious vigor and determination of one who believes in his divinity, will never do great things, because he will never make the demand that will draw a "sure supply."

Before one can hope to win out in any undertaking he must be able to say "I" positively, with the force of conviction. He must polarize his mind to the positive attitude. This is the attitude that creates, that produces results in the world of matter as well as in the realm of spirit.

The positive man is forceful because he has faith in himself. He forms his opinions without the aid of others and is not afraid to stand for what he thinks. He does not hesitate to differ with others. He is not a "mush of concession," like the negative weakling who subscribes to what everyone he meets says, thinks or believes. He makes statements with positiveness, without hesitation.

The Bible would never have gained such a dominating place in the life of the race had it referred to authorities to substantiate its statements; had it tried to prove its doctrines. Much of its supremacy has come from its tremendous positiveness, its vigorous affirmation of facts.

You will find nothing negative or wishy-washy in the Great Book. Its assertions are imperious, positive, dogmatic. It is one perpetual hammering, driving home of truths, of great fundamental facts. The Biblical writers speak with assurance and authority because of their profound conviction of the truths they utter. They do not argue or plead. They affirm. There is no appeal. As has been well said of the Bible, "It never appeals to readers for confirmation. It states. Every line breathes dominance, superiority and confidence."

We find the same imperious dominant qualities, the same positiveness in great leaders of men. They deal in affirmations. They throw themselves with intense conviction into whatever they attempt. They continually, both mentally and vocally, assert their power to do it, and—the result is a natural corollary; they succeed in what they attempt.

The difference between the positive and the negative mind, the man who can "assert the I" with vigor and the man who cannot, is the difference between success and failure.

The positive man keys his life to the "I can" note, the negative man to the "I can't."

The positive man denies the limitations of environment, of resources, of opportunities. He not only believes but knows that infinite bounty surrounds him, and that he can make it his own.

The negative man, on the other hand, will not fight against environment, no matter how hard it may be, but will yield to it without a struggle. He sees limitations and difficulties everywhere. To him obstacles are insurmountable.

But for the positive, dominant qualities in man we would still be living in caves and eating our food raw. It is the positive, forceful man that overcomes. Obstacles do not frighten, or turn him from his purpose. They are to him but the apparatus in the gymnasium, which give him additional strength and reinforce his determination to achieve. He knows that he can command infinite supply, that the great forces of the universe are working for him, and that he has only to direct them. He knows that it is his birthright to conquer; that the Creator put him here for that very purpose—to overcome, to grow, to ascend, to be godlike.

Every one has sufficient positive power to guide and direct his own life if he will only use and develop that power. If he does not use he will lose. If you do not think and act for yourself, if you do not assert yourself and push your own way, the forces about you will take command and push you. And remember this: When you are pushed you go down-hill; when you push yourself you go up-hill. Every one is either pusher or pushed in this world. Even the kingdom of heaven is taken by violence. He who would attain it must be aggressive for truth. No namby-pamby weakling who is afraid to stand on his own feet and fight for the right can get there.

If you ever expect to do anything to justify your existence, quit looking for some outside agent which will move your life train. Your power is coiled up right inside of you. There is where your engine is. The name of that engine is I. Use the great force at your command. Get up steam and forge ahead. You will never get very far by any other means. You are only losing time in trying to get any power outside of yourself, in pulls or influence, to move you forward. When the Creator made you a co-partner in His work, He put inside of you all the machinery necessary for the part you were to play. Claim what He intended for you. Develop and use your machinery, and no power on earth can hold you back from the goal you set for yourself.

Say to yourself, "It is my duty to make good, to obey that inner urge, that ambition prod which ever bids me up and on. I am resolved never again to allow anything to interfere with the free and untrammeled exercise of my physical and mental faculties. I will unfold all the possibilities that the Creator has infolded in the ego, the I of me. There is no lost day in God's calendar, no allowance for waste, and I am determined henceforth to make the most of the stuff that has been given me, to play the part of a son of Omnipotence."

As a matter of fact, every day has a splendid possible prize awaiting every human being, a prize which no money can buy. It can be obtained only at the price of splendid effort and self-assertion. We are too timid, too fearful of results even to attempt what we long to do. And we are too easy with ourselves, too willing to drift with the tide of our moods. Every man who has ever achieved grandly has been a stern schoolmaster to himself. He has incessantly affirmed his ideal and held himself unwaveringly to its realization.

By cultivating the positive we drive out the negative. This is a psychological law. It is to "empty by filling." Affirmation is always more potent than negation.

Prof. Halleck says "By restraining of an emotion, we can frequently throttle it; by inducing an expression, we can often cause its allied emotions."

Prof. Wm. James makes a similar statement. "Refuse to express a passion," he says, "and it dies. Count ten before venting your anger and its occasion seems ridiculous. Whistling to keep up courage is no mere figure of speech. On the other hand, sit all day in a moping posture, sigh, and reply to everything with a dismal voice, and your melancholy lingers. There is no more valuable precept in moral education than this, as all of us who have experienced know. If we wish to conquer undesirable emotional tendencies in ourselves we must assiduously, and in the first instance cold-bloodedly, go through the outward movements of those contrary dispositions which we wish to cultivate. Smooth the brow, brighten the eye, contract the dorsal rather than the ventral aspect of the frame, and speak in a major key, pass the genial compliment and your heart must indeed be frigid if it does not gradually thaw."

Few of us realize the tremendous force there is in the vigorous incessant affirmation of conditions which we long to establish. United with the visualizing of the man or woman we yearn to be or the thing we are determined to achieve, it becomes an irresistible power in shaping events. Act the part, affirm the possession, the assured realization of the thing desired, and it will tend to materialize. This is a fundamental law of creation.

What is called auto-suggestion, or self-suggestion, is one of the most active agencies employed in mind building. We can literally make our minds, thought by thought, as we can our bodies, fiber by fiber, through vigorous affirmation.

There is a mysterious power in the spoken word which gets a greater hold upon us than simply passing the same word through the mind or looking at it on the printed page. The vocal expression of a thought makes a greater impression upon the memory and especially influences the subconscious mind. It works like a leaven in the whole nature, putting agents in motion that establish a connection between us and our desires, the objects for which we are working. The persistent affirmation of our ability to do that which we have undertaken in a superb, kingly fashion, is a great stimulus, a positive, creative force.

There is nothing more helpful in building a strong positive character than bracing yourself up by searching, heart to heart talks with yourself. In this way, better perhaps than in any other, you can take stock of your mental assets and improve yourself all along the line.

If you are timid, for instance, or even feel that you are something of a coward, stoutly deny it. Insist that you are no shirker, no coward, that you are brave even to daring. Boldly assume the quality of a hero, vehemently affirm that you actually possess invincible courage, and you will be surprised at your immediate increase of strength and positiveness. Deny that you have any weakness, defect or deficiency which can handicap your career. Insist upon affirming the opposite quality, the winning quality.

If you lack decision, if you are a waverer, a vacillator, if you are a putter-off of things, if procrastination runs in your blood, persistently affirm that you possess the opposite qualities. At the same time resolve that you are going not only to play the heroic part in life, that you are not only going to begin work upon the duty awaiting you, but that you are going to put it through, that you are going to do things, and that you will never again allow yourself to waver, to procrastinate in the smallest matter, even if you do make mistakes now and then. Better make a mistake and forge ahead than to remain negative and inactive.

The habit of vigorous affirmation is the habit of victory. But remember that action must follow on the heels of resolution or you will never go any farther. Affirmation and resolution without prompt endeavor for realization are worse than useless. It is the man of action, of continued and repeated action, the man who never acknowledges defeat who ultimately wins out.

During our Civil War the Southern generals said it didn't do any good to beat Grant, because he never knew when he was beaten and, consequently, wouldn't stay beaten.

Men who leave their mark on the world are men of iron resolution, of grim determination. If youth were only taught at home and in school the power of an inflexible resolve, an inexorable affirmation of the thing they are determined to accomplish; if they were only taught the invincibleness of an unshakable will, of the positive victorious mental attitude, of a resolve which knows no defeat, life would not be half so hard.

"Nerve us with incessant affirmatives. Don't bark against the bad, but chant the beauties of the good." The positive, creative, affirmative elements are our friends. They draw us our sure supply. All negatives are our enemies. They drive away supply. Affirm the good, never the bad; the bright, never the dark; the true, and never the false; harmony, never discord. We should never forget that whatever tends to optimism is ready to "give us a lift."

The first step toward a happy, successful life is to get control of the supply that is ready to flow in answer to our demand. This you can do by forming the habit of affirming that the best will come to you, that only the things that are good for you can come into your life. Don't let yourself slip into the foolish habit of anticipating trouble, misfortune, sickness, disaster, accidents. To anticipate or expect such things is to affirm their reality and draw them to you. The habit of anticipating them will get them into the habit of "arriving." You will thus be drawn into a current of circumstance corresponding to the character of your negative thought.

Put yourself into a positive, success and happiness attitude the first thing every morning by taking time, even if only a few minutes, to commune with the Creator. Get into tune with the Infinite, the Source of your strength, the moment you awake. Keep yourself in harmony with the Principle which underlies your being during the day and your every act will be a step forward on the desired road.

Say to yourself constantly, "Happiness is my birthright. I was made to exult in life, not to go about with a long, sad, dejected face as though it had been a bitter disappointment, as though I were a misfit in the world. I was made to radiate joy and gladness and to go through life as a conqueror. If I am indeed a child of the Creator (and I know that I am), it is a positive insult to Him to go through the world as though I were a beggar, a slave. I bear the image of the King of kings, and it is my business to make all men see the likeness. It is my duty to prove my divine heritage by radiating royal manhood."

I know of no practice which will do more for one's growth and life-enlargement than the habit of rising above one's moods and discouragements through perpetual affirmation of one's divinity. If, for example, you get up in the morning feeling negative, blue and discouraged; if you don't feel like working at anything, just go off alone and have a good heart to heart talk with yourself something like this: "Now, look here, young man (or young woman), none of this: you are going to do a grand day's work to-day; you are going to get right out of this condition; you have had enough of it. If you are a real man (or woman) you will rise above your mood and wring victory out of this day, even though it looks so unpromising.

"It does not matter what comes or what goes, what happens or what does not happen, there is one thing I am sure of, and that is, I am going to be positive, creative, to get the most possible out of to-day; I am not going to allow anything to rob me of my happiness, or of my right to live this day through from beginning to end, and not merely to exist.

"I do not care what comes, I shall not allow any annoyance, any happening, any circumstance which may cross my path to rob me of my power and peace of mind. I will not be unhappy to-day, no matter what occurs. I am going to enjoy it to its fullest capacity. This shall be a complete day in my life. I shall not allow the enemies of my happiness to mar it. No misfortune in the past, nothing which has happened to me in days gone by, which has been disagreeable or tragic, no enemies of my efficiency, shall be guests in my spirit's

100

sacred enclosure to-day. Only happy thoughts, joy thoughts, friend thoughts shall find entertainment in my soul this day. No negative thoughts, none of my enemies shall gain admittance to scrawl their hideous autographs on the walls of my mind. There shall be 'no admittance' to-day, except to the friends of my best moods. I will tear down all black, sable pictures and hang in their place pictures of joy and gladness, of things which will encourage, cheer, and increase my power. Everything which ever handicapped my life, which has made me uncomfortable and unhappy, shall be expelled from my mental kingdom this day and every coming day."

If you make a resolve like this every morning and live up to it during the day, you cannot help being positive, productive, creative.

The positive mind repels all thought enemies that would hinder progress. Doubt, fear, despair, worry, these have no place in the creative brain. They are products of the negative mind. The man who would bend circumstances to his will can not afford to harbor them.

Hold negative, despondent, discouraged thoughts and your surroundings will be negative, unpropitious. Hold positive, confident, hopeful, cheerful thoughts and a congenial environment will manifest itself.

It is wonderful what right thinking can accomplish even in a naturally weak, negative mind. The insistent and persistent holding of the positive thought, the assurance thought, the self-confidence, the self-faith thought; the determined effort to think and act for oneself, to direct one's own forces will gradually change a negative non-productive mentality into a positive, creative one.

I have known very timid, sensitive people who scarcely dared to say their souls were their own before others, to so cure their habit of self-effacement and so strengthen their weak self-confidence by constant audible affirmation of their own strength, that in a very few months they had largely overcome this weakness.

Fear is negative; courage is positive, affirmative. If we would make our lives effective, we must root out all of the things which keep us in discord, all negative elements, and give ourselves over to the power of affirmation.

Many a person has ruined his life effort by depreciating it and sending out to those about him the negative vibration of his inferiority. We radiate our faith, our confidence in ourselves or our doubts, and distrust. Others catch the contagion of our opinion of ourselves.

Whatever you do, don't set up in your own mind and in that of others a picture of your self as a weak, ineffective, negative

101

personality. People do not realize the harm they do by making uncomplimentary and unfavorable remarks about themselves. It does not matter what it may be, the assertion of anything unfavorable to us or unlike what we wish to be is injurious. How often we hear men and women say: "I never can remember anything. I am always forgetting umbrellas and packages. I never can remember names or faces," and similar negative, depreciatory remarks. It never occurs to them that by making such statements as these they are strengthening their defects. They are not aware that by impressing these unfortunate images of themselves upon their mental mirror they are seriously injuring their self-confidence, their ultimate chance of being what they would like to be or of getting what they desire.

The character of civilization would be radically changed in a short time if parents were to teach their children the wonderful, strengthening, character-building power in the habit of affirmation. If boys and girls were impressed with the truth that the constant affirming of the good, the beautiful and the true, the insistent holding of the ideal of themselves as they would like to be, is a real creative force that tends to actualize what they long for many of the problems of the race would be solved.

As a matter of fact the worst enemy, as well as the best friend, any human being ever has is inside of him. The very mental attitude of the majority of people is utterly antagonistic to their advancement.

A really brainy professional man whom I meet quite often is a striking example of the baneful effects of the negative self-depreciatory thought. He wanted to do something big in his line, but he has had only mediocre success, and in consequence has so soured on life that he seems to have lost the power to enjoy himself. The truth is, the early contracted habit of self-castigation and unfavorable comparison with others who were more fortunate at the start has stayed by him through the years and practically disqualified his mind for real enjoyment or for making the most of his talents.

Another negative character of this type is a man in commercial life who is forever recalling his lack of opportunities. He never tires of referring to the fact that he was handicapped at his very birth by a slovenly slipshod father, and that all through life he has been placed at a great disadvantage compared with other men. He believes, and constantly affirms that he is unlucky, that he has never been at the right spot at the right time, that no matter how hard he works he feels a mysterious something holding him back.

Some malignant fate, or destiny, he complains, is always tripping him up, thwarting his most strenuous efforts, overturning his best laid plans. Through its machinations, although he has worked harder than anybody else he knows, he and his family have remained in poverty, while his associates have become prosperous.

The cause of this man's failure is not far to seek. It is plain that he started wrong and has been going wrong ever since. He has been talking failure all his life, affirming hard times, poverty, ill luck, and disappointment. He has been sowing thistles and all sorts of ill weeds in his garden and yet he wonders why his harvests have been so stingy, so blighted and over-shadowed by weeds.

Affirmations, acts, motives, ambitions, mental attitudes are the seeds sown in human gardens. Their character determines what our harvests shall be. Our future reaping depends entirely on our past sowing. What we are enjoying or suffering to-day is the result of yesterday's sowing. We are reaping weeds, thistles, thorns, or beautiful flowers and luscious fruit, according to the seeds we have sown.

The only soil in which our good seed thoughts will flourish is that of mental harmony. In this fruitful ground lies the secret of all efficiency and happiness. To come into unity with the Author of our being is to realize perfect mental harmony. And this is the first requisite of an efficient life, a goal that can be reached only by the road of constant, unfailing affirmation.

When you long for something that it is perfectly legitimate for you to have, sow your affirmation seed in perfect confidence that it will bloom in reality. Say to yourself, "Our Father-Mother-God is no respecter of persons. He is not partial in his treatment of His children. They all have the same rights, the same privileges. He will give me through my own effort what I need, what I ask for. The poorest, most ragged wretch that crawls has just as many hours in his day as has the ermined king. I can and I will do what I long to do. I will be what I desire to be." Affirm this again and again to yourself. Do not wait for an opportunity, make your opportunity. The power of affirmation will work miracles for you.

Most people seem to think that if they were only in an ideal environment, without worry or anxiety regarding the living-getting problem, if they were free from pain and in vigorous health, they would then be perfectly happy. But, as a matter of fact, we are not half so dependent for happiness upon environment, upon circumstances, as we imagine we are. False ambition, envy and jealousy are responsible for much of our uneasiness, our restlessness and discontent. Our minds are so intent upon what other people have and are doing that we do not get a tithe of the enjoyment and satisfaction out of our own work, out of our own possessions, that they should afford us. We think so much about what others have and spend so much time wondering why we cannot have similar things that we do not see the beauty, loveliness and sweetness in our own environment. We question and envy when we should affirm and realize. We neglect the most potent means within our grasp—the miracle-working power of affirmation. The supply will come in answer to our demand.

Every one of us has an inalienable right to be comfortable, prosperous, free from anxiety,—in short to be happy. Man was not intended to be a worrying machine. The fundamental principle of the human constitution is based on harmony and, when we are in harmonious relations with the universe, we attain the maximum of efficiency, of power, of usefulness to the world. It is then we get the maximum of enjoyment and happiness out of life. Is it not worth while to get into such relations? Is it not foolish to remain in discord when by the simple process of affirmation, linked with divine faith and effort, we can transform ourselves and our environment?

CHAPTER XI

THE TRIUMPH OF HEALTH IDEALS

"What is the body after all but the spirit breaking through the flesh, or health but beauty in the organism?"
Every good emotion makes a health and life promoting change in the body. Every thought is registered in the brain by a physical change more or less permanent in the tissue cells.
The coming man will find it as easy to counteract an unfriendly, vicious thought by turning on the counter thought to neutralize it, as to rob the hot water of its burning power by turning on the cold water faucet.
There is a divine something in man which never was sick and never can be, that divine self, the image of the Creator, perfect, unchangeable, indestructible, immortal, and which some time and somewhere must drive out all trace of sin, disease and death in mankind.

Hufeland.

Even those who do not believe in Christian Science as a whole must be impressed with the Scientists' wonderful religious optimism. Their inspiring mental attitude, the hopeful way in which they face life, always looking toward the light, toward health, toward prosperity, toward success, and turning their backs upon the darkness, upon everything which can mar their health, their efficiency, their happiness, is creating a new world for thousands of discouraged souls.

Christian Scientists insist that since God has created everything that is, and since He is perfect, is all-in-all, He could not possibly create anything unlike Himself, such as disease, or anything else which is not good for His children. God is harmony, they reason, and He could not create discord. He is truth and He could not create error. God is love and He could not create the opposite of love,— hatred, jealousy, envy, selfishness, any evil emotion or passion. Hence all disease, all discord, all the enemies of the race, all Satanic influences in the world must be accounted for in some other way than as decrees of His will, for Perfection could not have produced these imperfections. Love could not create anything antagonistic to itself.

Scientists take a positive and vigorous stand against the

admission to their mind of any of the enemies of their health, their prosperity, their happiness or their destiny. Not only is all thought of failure and poverty banished, but they close the portals of their mind against fear, worry and anxiety, against the ravages of jealousy, the poison of hatred, envy, and selfishness. They try to keep their mental realm clear of all black, forbidding pictures, of all sorts of distressing emotions and unfriendly thoughts, while they open it wide to the things which help, inspire and bring hope, the friend thoughts and emotions,—joy, gladness, love, truth, and divine inspiration.

They believe that all human beings were not only made to be healthy but also to be happy, successful, prosperous. They regard poverty, no less than illness, as a mental disease, to be treated in the same manner as bodily disease; and this cheerful religious optimism which they try steadily to maintain is not alone a healing force, but is also a great disease-resisting power.

Health, wholeness, is one of the most important and necessary factors for the attainment of those things which every normal human being desires,—peace, power, plenty, success and happiness. The Scientists' religious optimism is a potent force for placing the mind in the most favorable condition for the attainment of all these things. It removes all hindrances to full, complete self-expression.

It is just as necessary to hold the victorious attitude toward health as it is to hold the victorious attitude toward our career and everything which affects it. It is just as necessary to get rid of our doubts and fears regarding our physical well-being, as it is to get rid of our doubts and fears regarding our ability to succeed.

If we would be strong and vigorous it is quite as important to visualize health, to hold the health ideal, to keep the perfect health picture constantly in the mind, as it is to keep the prosperity, the success ideal in the mind when we are striving for an independence.

The habit of always holding a high ideal of our health, of thinking of ourselves as well, vigorous, physically and mentally perfect, will go very far toward building up a strong disease-resisting barrier between ourselves and all our health enemies. On the other hand, people who never think of themselves as whole, healthy, active and robust, but who constantly hold in mind a picture of themselves as weak, ailing, without vim or stamina, with little or no disease-resisting power, are liable at any time to become victims of disease. The building up of a strong health thought barrier, a vigorous health conviction between ourselves and disease is the best sort of health insurance. Fearing disease, thinking ill health, visualizing physical suffering, is the surest way of attracting those things.

Physicians know that the awful incubus of doubt and worry in the minds of patients, the fear that their disease may be fatal, is the greatest obstacle to their recovery. We head toward our doubts, our fears, our convictions regarding our health, just as we do toward our doubts, fears and convictions regarding other things. If we are convinced that we are not going to be strong, rugged, virile, if we fear that we are likely to develop inherited weaknesses and disease tendencies, we are headed toward these conditions, and will probably realize them. On the contrary, if we hold the victorious attitude toward health, if we visualize the health ideal, the health conviction, we head mentally toward health, and what we head toward mentally is the pattern of that which is continually being built into our life structure.

A healthy body is healthy thought externalized.

Man's normal condition is that of robust health, vigorous vitality, tremendous power of endurance. The Creator evidently intended the human machine to run harmoniously, without friction, without weakness or disability of any kind.

The created is a part of the Creator, an indestructible part of Him. When we rise to a full consciousness of this we shall be victors over disease instead of victims of it; we shall be conquerors instead of slaves of conditions.

Nearly a century ago a celebrated German physician said that there is something in man which was never born, is never sick and never dies, and that it is this something, this omnipotent force within which in reality heals our diseases. No matter what we may call it, this something that repairs and renews is one with the Force that creates us. We may name it variously the God principle, the Christ within us, the divine principle, the omnipotent force or anything else we please; the name does not matter. All mean the same thing, that is, the creative, the all-sustaining Force that holds the universe in harmony.

There is something in you that is lord over your physical organs. There is a power in you, back of the flesh, but not of it, which dominates the flesh, and that is the real you. Your partner in that power is the Intelligence that created you. You are indissolubly interlinked with that Intelligence. You can no more be wiped out of existence than the Creator who made you, because you are an immortal expression of Himself. You are His masterpiece, and His work must partake of His qualities, of His perfection, of His omnipotence, of His omniscience.

The trouble with us is we do not rise to the power and dignity of our divinity. We do not half believe we are divine. We have a sort of vague theory that we are mere puppets, thrown off as separate units into space, without any vital connection with the Power that gave us life. This false theory is the cause of our sufferings.

The reason why we are such shriveled, scrub oaks of human beings is found in the dried-up, mean, stingy ideal of ourselves which we have been taught to hold. We have been reared to think of ourselves as "poor miserable worms of the dust," unworthy to come into the presence of our Father-Mother-God, even though we are fashioned in His image. Instead of carrying through life an ideal of our mental and physical perfection, we carry an ideal of a defective, diseased, physically and mentally imperfect, being. The mind being the molder of the body, the life-giving processes within us build the sort of body that answers to the model in the mind, the ideal which we hold of ourselves. What we really believe ourselves to be, we tend to become. We keep our minds filled with all sorts of discordant, sick pictures, and of course all of these mental images reappear in the body, react upon the life.

On the other hand, every time we affirm that we are one with the creative Force of the universe, that nothing can separate us from our oneness with the One, we tend to build our bodies into the ideal state of perfect health,—mental, physical, and moral wholeness. If we could hold continually the ideal of our wholeness, and visualize ourselves as perfect beings "even as He is perfect," and constantly try to live up to our ideal, any tendency to imperfection, to discord, to disease would be eliminated.

We are only just beginning to realize the tremendous import of the idea that we really fashion our bodies to correspond with our thoughts, that we are co-creators of ourselves with the Divine Power which is back of the flesh, but not of it.

A prominent surgeon in speaking of infantile paralysis says that the physician's mental attitude toward it has a great deal to do with its cure, and that he should hold firmly in mind the idea that the disease is curable.

Every physician should also be a metaphysician. He should be a profound believer in the principle that the Power which created the patient can re-create him, can repair damages, restore diseased or lost tissues. The most advanced physicians do believe that at best they can but help Nature in her healing processes. They realize that the same Power which created the patient is present in the healing of every wound, every broken bone and every hurt we suffer. The surgeon sets the bone, dresses the wound, but the same Power that first created the flesh and bone must do the healing.

The mental healer vigorously denies the reality of disease in the sense that truth is a reality. To him "all is Infinite Mind, and its infinite manifestation," as Mrs. Eddy says, and therefore all must be good. Only the good can be real as God made all that is.

The persistent denial that anything could exist which the Creator did not create, and that He could make anything unlike Himself, is one of the fundamental principles of the Christian Science faith. To the healer health is a vital, immortal principle, the everlasting fact, and disease, although it seems painfully real to the sufferer, is but a false belief.

The healer holds in mind only what he desires to establish in his patient's mind. He shuts out everything else. Health is what he wishes to establish, and to do this he holds insistently and tenaciously the health ideal. He refuses to see the sick, diseased man or woman, and persists in visualizing the ideal one that God intended. To him the defective, deficient, suffering being which disease and physical discord have made is not the real man or woman. That being is only a travesty of the ideal, perfect creature the Creator planned.

He does not allow himself to think of, or to picture disease symptoms. To visualize the physical appearance of disease would be to acknowledge its reality, and this would be to defeat his healing. He could not, for example, cure cancer or tuberculosis while mentally picturing the horrible symptoms of these diseases. He wishes to keep all such things out of his mind because of their baleful suggestiveness. Visualizing them would merely etch their reality deeper and deeper in his consciousness, and the suggestion would be conveyed into the patient's consciousness.

The mental healer's aim is to produce in the mind of the person he is treating a consciousness of the scientific reality of health, and of the unreality of disease. It does not matter how the disease symptoms may contradict this principle, or how loudly pain may scream for recognition, he persists in considering disease unreal and in holding the scientific sense of health as the reality. He relies wholly upon Divine Mind as the great healing potency, and steadily affirms his patient's oneness with his Divine Source, and that disease cannot exist in the Divine Presence.

At the very outset he encourages his patient by affirming that, however real his physical discord or disease may seem to him, it cannot affect the God image in him, because that is perfect, as God Himself is perfect, and that in reality there can be no disease. Truth and harmony, he asserts, are the great facts of life. Error is not a reality, but merely the absence of truth; discord is not a reality, but merely the absence of harmony. He assures him that He is God's child, and that God's image cannot be sick, distressed or diseased.

"Of course," he says, "this seems very real to you, painfully real, but it is not reality in the sense that truth is a reality." This is discord, the absence of harmony, and divine harmony will antidote all discord just as truth will neutralize error, and as love will neutralize all hatred, jealousy or revenge, or as confidence, self-assurance will neutralize fear, doubt, or self-depreciation.

The healer holds continually the healing suggestions, and concentrates on arousing in his patient expectancy of relief by bracing his hope, confidence, assurance and faith in Divine Mind that restores, renews and heals. He tries to stimulate and to put into active operation the healing potencies latent in him, to awaken in his mind the lost divine image, and to impress upon him the idea that this divine image cannot possibly be dominated or in any way affected by disease.

I have seen a chemist pour a few drops of liquid from different crucibles into a jar of muddy water and in a few minutes the mud would disappear and the water be as pure as crystal. This is in effect what the mental healer does in treating a patient. No matter what the disease is his great remedy lies in mental chemistry, in neutralizing, destroying the error with its natural antidote.

The healer's constant affirmation that there can be no sickness, no disease in God's image in man, is a powerful suggestion which tends to weaken the grip of error in his patient's body. The very shutting out of all fear, of the terror of disease and death, is a great step towards a cure, because these things are depressing to all the bodily functions. Everything that discourages, that makes the patient despondent, is a great devitalizer, and constantly lowers his disease-resisting power.

The arousing of the belief that the healer is a sort of motorman who puts up the patient's dropped trolley pole, thus making connection with the wire carrying infinite power; or that he is a wireless operator who is connecting him with his Divine Source, the source of health and happiness, and that he is actually receiving the flow of divine force, of peace, of immortal life, is of itself a tremendous healing agency.

When he has succeeded in establishing in the mind of his patient the vigorous conviction that health is the everlasting principle, the great fundamental inviolable fact, the healer has gone far toward establishing a scientific consciousness of health, and has laid a most important health foundation.

After a little practice a sick person can do wonderful things for himself through the vitalizing force of auto-suggestion. He can be his own physician. He can recover health and keep it by applying to himself the same principles that the healer applies to his patient. In this way he can keep himself in conscious union with the Divine Source of all supply, of all good, all health.

There are sufficient latent potencies in every human being, if he would only arouse and make them operative, to keep him in health and harmony. We can all be our own healers if we will.

The stream must be as pure as its fountain head unless contaminated later, and there is where we humans come in. We contaminate the health stream with our thought poisons. Our doubts, our fears, our unbeliefs, our brutal passions, our selfishness, our greed, our hatreds, our jealousies, our revenge, our ingratitude for life, for the blessings we enjoy,—all of these things tend to pollute the stream which we receive pure as it flows from the crystal fountain, the divine source of the All Good.

But the practice of divine chemistry will enable us to clear up our muddy life streams. We have in ourselves the remedies which will neutralize the vicious poisons we have allowed to flow into and befoul our life stream. We can by the right use of our powers purify it as the chemist purified the jar of muddy water. By right thinking we can neutralize the poison sewage of our bodies, just as chemists can take the foul sewage water which flows out from a city and by the help of chemicals neutralize all the filth, making it absolutely pure again. By applying their antidotes we can neutralize the poisons of disease, the results of wrong thinking and living, which sap and embitter our lives, which make us suffer from all sorts of ills and leave us unable to accomplish one-tenth of what we might if we had that splendid physical and mental vigor which is normal to humanity.

We must offer the same uncompromising opposition to the reality of all kinds of disease, mental and physical, that the mental healer does. We must see ourselves as he sees his patient, in the wholeness, the completeness, the Creator intended. It is the ideal man or woman we must visualize, never the one weakened, deformed by horrible diseases or their symptoms. By recognizing only the real man or woman, unaffected by wrong thinking, we cut off the vicious effects of the mental enemies which are fighting to perpetuate disease or other unfortunate conditions.

The constant holding of the health ideal, of the truth thought, the health and prosperity thought, the optimistic thought, the kindly, cheerful, helpful thought and the shutting out of all their opposites, not only help to restore health, but also increase tremendously the disease-resisting power. Right thought is a health, efficiency, and happiness tonic.

The vital thing in establishing health is to adopt the victorious attitude toward it as toward every other good thing we desire. If we wish to have abounding health (and who does not?) we must cultivate implicit faith in health as our birthright, in the truth that, being the children of Perfection, we must partake of the qualities of perfection, and hence be free from the imperfection of disease or sickness.

Without faith in our wholeness we are not, and cannot be, whole. Without faith in the healing power of Divine chemistry no healing is possible either by patient or healer. The patient may not always have a conscious faith, but the healer has, and a similar faith is aroused in the patient later, as he begins to feel the divine healing power operating and working like a leaven in his nature.

There is no one thing that is emphasized so much in the Bible, and especially in Christ's teachings as faith. Every benefit, every healing depends for its efficacy on the sufferer's faith. In all of His healing this one condition of faith was imperative—"According to thy faith be it unto thee."

When the disciples told their Master that they could not heal certain cases He rebuked them, and told them that they failed because of their lack of faith. "According to thy faith be it unto thee," he reiterated constantly. He recognized the great healing power of faith, and impressed upon His followers the truth, that without it no healing was possible.

Every physician knows that his patient's faith in his power to cure him, in the efficacy of the remedies he applies, are curative agencies. Faith in medicinal remedies is what makes them effective. It is faith that furnishes the potency of thousands of so-called remedies, which have no intrinsic value whatever.

We all know how the visualizing of disease and the fear of it affect the mind in undermining the health ideal. Confidence in our health is really its sustaining and buttressing power, for the moment we destroy this we lessen our resisting power and invite disease.

The image perpetually held in the conscious mind becomes indelibly etched in the subconscious mind and the body conforms to the thought. To attain perfect health we must hold the image of physical perfection, we must constantly keep in mind this ideal state. We must build ourselves thought pictures of a superb body in all its strength and wholeness; we must relentlessly strangle every image of weakness or disease, every sick suggestion that would blur the picture of perfect wholeness and harmony into which we wish to grow.

What a revolution we would make in our lives if we could only learn to live this health ideal instead of its opposite, the disease ideal!

Every child should be reared to think health instead of disease; should be made to realize that health is the everlasting fact, that disease is not a necessary evil, and was not intended for us, that it was not intended we should suffer. If the young mind were saturated from infancy with health ideas and ideals it would build up a strong disease-resisting power that would make it immune to all health enemies. If every child were trained to believe that he was a god in the making, that he had within him the embryo of divinity which ought to develop into a God-like being, we should not have so many mental and physical Lilliputians.

One of our great health troubles lies in the fact that we have been accustomed from childhood to lay too much emphasis on matter, on the support of the body. As a matter of fact, the mind is everything. But mind is not confined to the head alone. We are all mind. We think all over. We live all over. Our sensations are the intelligent expression of all the cells of the body.

The body is a great coöperative institution composed of billions of cells. Some of these cells have a higher functioning quality than others, but they all have their appointed places. Every cell is an important member of the body corporation and has a voice in the government of the whole. When we are wounded or diseased, for instance, billions of these tiny cell repairers, healers, renewers, health builders, rush instantly to the wounded part to repair and restore the injured tissues.

We are all conscious that there is continually going on within us these repairing, renewing, reinvigorating, as well as healing, processes. We feel that there is a marvelous and beneficent intelligence ever working miracles within us, a power which heals our wounds and cures our hurts.

Whence comes the intelligence which governs and directs the work of these little builders and repairers? It comes from the Within of us, for our objective mind is comparatively passive in the process. But the great Intelligence back of the flesh, which keeps the heart beating, the lungs breathing, and all of the various bodily functions in activity, never ceases working, and never leaves us for an instant. It permeates every atom of the body, illuminating each separate cell with a reflection of its own light.

Scientists are making marvelous discoveries regarding the location of the seat of intelligence,—mind. Until recently it was supposed to be confined solely to the brain. But now we know the mind, the brain, or the thinking part of us, extends the entire length of the spinal cord, that there is gray brain matter everywhere in the sympathetic nervous system. In fact recent experiments indicate selective power in the cells all through the body.

Regular gray matter has been found in the finger tips of deaf, dumb and blind people, thus showing that wherever there is a need there is intelligence. We know what marvels blind and deaf mutes perform by their sense of touch, in distinguishing colors, even fine variations of shades in delicate fabrics, in correctly sensing denominations of paper money and coins, and accurately describing statues and other forms from merely running their fingers over them. This shows that intelligence is everywhere in the body.

Some of our foremost scientists now believe that the cells composing each organ form a sort of coöperative community intelligence which presides over that particular organ. They hold that the bodily organs have what may be termed minds of their own, and are vitally connected with the so-called spinal column brain and the solar plexus brain, as well as with the brain proper. This theory is borne out in fact. We know how quickly the stomach sympathizes with the mental attitude, how it responds to our thoughts, our emotions; also how quickly the heart, the kidneys respond to our mental states—fear, worry, joy, anxiety, love, hate, jealousy, whatever emotion dominates us.

If there were not a very intimate connection between the brain and the stomach (and the same principle applies to the heart, the kidneys and other organs) the digestion would not be affected so seriously by our changing moods and emotions. Inasmuch as it is so affected, is it not reasonable to assume that the stomach cells are influenced by the thought which you project into them? Is it not reasonable to assume that by sending into these cells black, gloomy, discouraging pictures of indigestion and dyspepsia you injuriously affect them? If these cells have intelligence, and if they respond instantly to our different mental states, as we know they do, isn't it natural that they should be correspondingly affected by our opinion of them, by our lack of confidence in them, our suspicion of their ability to digest our food properly, by our constant complaining of our stomach and our miserable digestive apparatus?

Give a dog a bad name and you might as well kill him, is an old saying. In the same way, impress, force home on your stomach, your heart, your liver, or any other bodily organ the conviction that it is inefficient, weak, good for nothing, and in addition swallow a mouthful of mental dyspepsia with every mouthful of food, and, sooner or later, it will accept your verdict and be just what you claim it is.

In other words, instead of handicapping them by wrong thought, we must give our bodily organs a fair chance to do their legitimate work. If we expect them to act perfectly, as the Creator intended they should, we must treat them as we would treat our children. We must by right thinking help them to be normal instead of making them abnormal by doubting, being suspicious of them. We must visualize them as our co-workers, our partners, our friends, not as our enemies, our tormentors.

Just think of the horrible pictures of their various organs people get from medical books, which describe minutely symptoms of diseases which they imagine they have! Many people never visualize a normal picture of themselves. They never think of themselves as the perfect beings God intended them to be. What they hold constantly in mind is a picture of an abnormal, diseased, weak, defective creature. They picture their stomach, their liver, their kidneys, their heart in a diseased, imperfect condition. Instead of regarding them as friends, as members of the same family, they look on them as malicious enemies who cause them constant suffering. "Oh," they cry out, "I've got such a miserable stomach! I can't eat anything. Everything I eat hurts me." "My treacherous old heart, how it pumps. I can't walk or do any of the things I like because of it." "My liver is all upset. I seem to be out of kilter everywhere. My kidneys are affected, my back troubles me, and really I might as well be dead!"

Such horrible visualizing and belittling of the hard-working bodily organs would ruin the health of the best trained athlete. If you would be a friend to yourself, you must be a friend of your organs, which are so intimately and sympathetically connected with your brain-mind—the central station of your body. You must believe in their perfection, in their normal functioning. You must picture them trying to help you to carry out your great life purpose instead of working at cross purposes with you. You must have confidence in them, think of them as your friends instead of enemies handicapping your success and ruining your chances in life. Replace the pictures of diseased organs with their opposites, pictures of their wholeness, their completeness, their soundness, and you will find yourself coming into health and power.

Assume the victorious attitude, and think of yourself as an absolutely perfect being, divine, immortal, possessing superb health, a magnificent physique, a vigorous constitution, a sublime mind.

Every morning when you rise, before you go to bed at night, and whenever you think of it during the day, stoutly affirm the fact of

115

your perfection physically, mentally and morally. Constantly assert mentally, and, when alone, orally, "I am health because I am of God. God is my life, He is the great creative Power that sustains and upholds me every instant. This Power is perpetually re-creating me, and trying to keep me up to the ideal, the original plan of my being when I was created. I shall coöperate with it to-day, and every day. I shall aim to be perfect, even as my Father."

There is a great restorative power in the mere resolve to be well, strong and vigorous, in affirming and tenaciously holding the perfect ideal of ourselves which the Creator had in His plan of us. There is a re-creative force in the realization that any departure from this ideal means departure from God, from perfect health, from the reality of the perfect physical, mental and moral being planned by Him.

You will be surprised to see how this mental attitude, this visualized physical ideal, will be reproduced in the body.

The mind is the body builder, the great health sculptor, and we cannot surpass our mental model. If there is a weakness or flaw in the thought model, there will be corresponding deficiencies in the health statue. As long as we think ill health, doubt our ability to be strong and vigorous, as long as we hold the conviction of the presence of inherited weaknesses and disease tendencies, look upon ourselves as victims instead of conquerors of ill health, in short, as long as the mental model is defective perfect health is impossible.

Joyous, abounding health can be established just as anything else can be established, by right thinking and right living, by thinking health instead of disease, thinking strength instead of weakness, harmony instead of discord, thinking true thoughts instead of error thoughts, love thoughts instead of hatred thoughts, health thoughts, upbuilding thoughts instead of destructive tearing down thoughts.

A great many regular physicians now, and all soon will, show patients how they can make use of the great healing, medicinal power of thought, the miracle of right thinking, which unites them with the Force back of the flesh. They will show each patient what attitudes of mind, what affirmations and what auto-suggestions will tend to keep him in harmony; they will teach him the healing use of suggestion. The physician of the future will use largely for his remedies, ideas, mental attitudes, and suggestions.

The time will come when parents and teachers will realize the tremendous force, the character-building power in the affirmation of health, wholeness, completeness, harmony. They will teach children to exert this power that will drive out discord and dispel disease. They will impress upon the young that affirmation of

116

perfect ideals, holding in mind the model of a perfect man, a perfect woman, not the one marred, crippled, shorn of strength and beauty by violation of mental law, or by vicious living, will protect them from all assaults from without and from within.

If that mind was always in us which was in Christ, the mind that gives health, peace and happiness, that perpetuates harmony, truth and beauty, we should never know discord of any kind. Perfect health would be the rule and not the exception, because we should never transgress the laws of our being.

CHAPTER XII

YOU ARE HEADED TOWARD YOUR IDEAL

Faith and the ideal still remain the most powerful levers of progress and of happiness. Jean Finot.
If we are content to unfold the life within according to the pattern given us, we shall reach the highest end of which we are capable.
We tend to grow into the likeness of the things we long for most, think about most.
The gods we worship write their names on our faces.

Emerson.

In Hawthorne's story, "The Great Stone Face," we have an impressive illustration of the power of an ideal. One's memory holds a vivid picture of its hero, whose mind had dwelt from childhood on the local tradition that a man-child should be born whose face would resemble that of the mountain profile above the little hamlet of his nativity; and that this child would eventually become the leader and savior of the people. So whole-heartedly did he believe the legend, so earnestly did he long for its fulfillment, and so constantly did his eyes dwell on the prophetic profile, that unconsciously his own features changed until, outwardly as well as inwardly, he completely embodied the ideal which his mind had absorbed.

On every hand we see illustrations of the transforming power of the ideal. It is outpictured in the faces we see in the street, in trains and shops, in theaters and churches, wherever people congregate.

How quickly we can select from a crowd of strangers the successful business man. His initiative, leadership, executive ability, speak out of his face and manner. The same is true of men in other vocations,—of the scholar, the clergyman, the lawyer, the teacher, the doctor, the farmer, the day laborer. Go into any institution, factory, store, or other place of business and you can quickly detect the nature of the ideals outpictured in the faces, in the expression, in the manner of the people you see there. Visit Sing Sing and you will see the power of the ideal which has worked like a leaven in its inmates. The criminal suggestion, the criminal thought, the criminal ideal is reflected in the faces of those who visualized crime, planned and thought out its details long before they committed the criminal act.

Whatever we hold in our minds, dwell upon, contemplate, whatever is dominant in our motives, will stand out in our flesh so that the world can read it. Many absolutely authentic cases of stigmata are recorded in the lives of medieval saints, on whose bodies appeared an exact reproduction of all the wounds of the crucified Christ. Some of these cases were in convents and monasteries, and were the result of long and intense concentration of the mind of the subject upon the physical sufferings of Christ. Frequently the phenomena occurred after the austerities of Lent, during which the monks and nuns had focused more intensely and steadily upon the tortures of the Savior's passion and death.

If the contemplation of those tortures, the constant mental picturing of the sufferings of the God-man, the soul's great sympathy with its ideal could change the very tissues of the body, could reproduce on it the actual physical marks of the cruel spear in the side, of the nails in the hands and feet and of the thorns in the head, think of the wonderful possibilities in the reversal of these thoughts and this picturing. Think of what the contemplation of the wonderful work accomplished by the Savior on earth, of the constant mental picturing of His glorious life, of His tenderness, and love for humanity, of His power and dignity, of His continual outpouring of Himself in service; think of what the constant holding of such an ideal, such a model, and the perpetual effort to realize it would do for the race!

We tend to become like what we admire, sympathize with and persistently hold in mind. The hero of "The Great Stone Face" became the counterpart of his ideal. The history of Christianity is a continuous record of the power of the ideal to raise men and women to their highest power. St. Paul, one of the most conspicuous of these examples, is so possessed, so enthused by the inspiration of his great model, that he cries, "I live, not I, but Christ in me."

"The contemplation of perfection is always uplifting." Nothing so strengthens the mind, enlarges manhood, or womanhood, widens the thought, as the constant effort to measure up to high ideals. The struggle to better our best, to make our highest moments permanent, the continual reaching of the mind to the things above and beyond, the steady pursuit of the ideal, which constantly advances as we pursue, is what has led the race up from savagery to twentieth century civilization.

A great artist was one day found by a friend in tears in his studio. When asked the cause of his distress, he replied, "I have produced a work with which I am satisfied, and I shall never produce another." It is said he never did. The inspiration that had urged him on was his ideal. That kept him always striving to improve on what he had previously done. Without it there was nothing to strive for.

Without an ideal there is no growth; and where there is no growth there is retrogression. Without a vision the people perish. Nothing in the universe is static. None of us stands still. We are all traveling in some direction, either forward or backward. Everything depends on the ideal.

What we admire and aspire to enters into the very texture of our being, becomes a part of us. If we had the power to analyze any individual, we could tell what books he had read, could detect the type of his friends and associates, and could name his heroes; that is, we could tell what ideals had actuated him.

Parents and teachers should urge upon the young the importance of hero worship, of choosing the highest human ideals. Our lives are molded chiefly after the pattern of the ideals of our youth, and there is no danger of too much hero worship, if only the heroes are worthy.

History is full of examples of the powerful influence of ideals upon our great men. It is said that Alexander the Great always carried a copy of Homer's "Iliad" in his pocket, and that he never tired of reading about Achilles, the great hero, whom he was ambitious to resemble. Many a young man in this country who has been inspired, encouraged and stimulated by Lincoln's career, has not only lived a grander life and made a truer success because he modeled his life after that of his hero, but he has developed many qualities in common with Lincoln which otherwise might have lain forever dormant. Many a young officer in our army is more efficient because of his imitation of Grant and Lee, the ideals which haunted his dreams and which have ever urged him up and on.

It is of the utmost importance to choose our ideal early in life, a high and beautiful ideal, that shall be our pole star, the highest, brightest light we know. A recent writer says: "My advice to all those just starting to travel life's turnpike is:

"Don't start until you have your ideal.
Then don't stop until you get it."

Of course we all have ideals of some kind when we are young; but how many of us keep them even till middle age? What young man has entered into active life without an ideal before him of what he is going to do, and how the world is going to be bettered by him? What young girl but who, leaving school, life smiling before her, dreams of the ideal love she will find, the ideal happy home she will make, and the beautiful work she will do in life with the ideal man of her girlish dreams by her side? But do the youth and the maiden hold these ideals throughout the years, with the strength of conviction that overcomes all difficulties, or do they abandon them with the first discouragement and settle down into a commonplace existence with interest in nothing above the material?

To youth, naturally, come glorious ideals, not only of what one's own life is to be, but of what life in general should be,—the ideal man, the ideal woman, the ideal social system,—and with all these is a vague desire or intention to help toward their fulfillment. But too often the result of disappointment in the effort to better conditions is, first, to give up the hope of realizing the ideal, and then to abandon the ideal itself. Here is where the great danger of retrogression comes in. Unless the ideal be held with a tenacity that no failure or disappointment can relax, it is apt to fade away after the first ardor of youth is past.

One of the greatest aids to the preservation of the youthful ideal in all its freshness and beauty is to recall frequently, daily, the moral heroes who first gave one a glimpse of one's possibilities and aroused one's ambition. Read the special books, or particular chapters which fired you to emulate some noble character. Renew yourself mentally by visualizing the life and work of men and women who have wrought nobly for humanity. Think of the Washingtons, the Franklins, the Lincolns, the Emersons, the Ruskins, the Florence Nightingales, the Jane Addams, the Susan B. Anthonys, the Frances Willards, and you will be strengthened to resist the debasing influence of the fierce competition for wealth and preferment, even for mere subsistence, which in so many instances pushes out of sight the aspirations and ideals of youth. Keep constantly in mind the grand characters whose achievements aroused you to noble thoughts and endeavor in the springtime of life and your standards will never drop. Character always develops according to the pattern within us. No artist could paint the face of Christ with the model of Judas before his mental vision. No great character can ever be built with low, groveling ideals in the mind.

The constant struggle to measure up to a high ideal is the only force in heaven or on earth that can make a life great, beautiful and fruitful. If we would ever accomplish anything of worth, if we would ever establish our oneness with the Creator, and accomplish the work He sent us here to do, we must live up to our ideal.

With eyes fixed on this ideal, we must work with heart and hand and brain; with a faith that never grows dim, with a resolution that never wavers, with a patience that is akin to genius, we must persevere unto the end; for, as we advance, our ideal as steadily moves upward.

"The situation that has not its duty, its ideal," says Carlyle, "was never yet occupied by man. Yes, here, in this poor, miserable, hampered, despicable Actual, wherein thou even now standest, here or nowhere is thy ideal; work it out therefrom, and, working, believe, live, be free. Fool! the ideal is in thyself."

Never were truer words spoken. Wrapped up in every human being there are divine energies which, if given proper direction, will develop the ideal from stage to stage. Who sees a sculptor at work upon a block of marble sees what appears to be only a mechanical performance. But, out of sight in the sculptor's brain, there is a quiet presence we do not perceive; and every movement of the hand is impelled by that shining thought within the brain. That presence is the ideal. Without it he would be a mason; through it he becomes an artist.

"The ideal is the real." By it we shape our lives as the sculptor shapes the image from the rough marble. External means alone will not accomplish this. You must lay hold of eternal principles, of the everlasting verities, or you never can approach your ideal. Your first advance toward it lies in what you are doing now, in what you are thinking. Not on some far-off height, in some distant scene, or fabled land, where longing without endeavor is magically satisfied, will we carve out the ideal that haunts our souls, but "here and now in this poor, mean Actual, here or nowhere is our ideal!"

In the humble valley, on the boundless prairie, on the farm, on sea or on land, in workshop, store, or office, wherever there is honest work for the hand and brain of man to do,—within the circumscribed limits of our daily duties, is the field wherein the outworking of our ideal must be wrought.

"Your circumstances may be uncongenial," says James Allen, "but they shall not long remain so if you but perceive an Ideal and strive to reach it. You cannot travel within and stand still without. Here is a youth hard pressed by poverty and labor; confined long hours in an unhealthy workshop; unschooled, and lacking all the arts of refinement. But he dreams of better things; he thinks of intelligence, of refinement, of grace and beauty. He conceives of, mentally builds up, an ideal condition of life; the vision of a wider liberty and a larger scope takes possession of him; unrest urges him to action, and he utilizes all his spare time and means, small though they are, to the development of his latent powers and resources. Very soon so altered has his mind become that the workshop can no longer hold him. It has become so out of harmony with his mentality that it falls out of his life as a garment is cast aside, and, with the growth of opportunities which fit the scope of his expanding powers, he passes out of it forever. Years later we see this youth as a full-grown man. We find him a master of certain forces of the mind which he wields with world-wide influence and almost unequaled power. In his hands he holds the cords of gigantic responsibilities; he speaks, and lo! lives are changed; men and women hang upon his words and remold their characters, and, sun-like, he becomes the fixed and luminous center round which innumerable destinies revolve. He has realized the Vision of his youth. He has become one with his Ideal."

The great curse of the average person is commonness,—the lack of aspiring ideals. There are thousands of farmers who never get above cattle and wheat, of doctors who never become superior to prescriptions and diseases, of lawyers who never wholly subordinate their briefs. The ideals of the masses rarely rise out of mediocrity. Most of us live in the basement of our lives, while the upper stories are all unused. Millions of human beings never get out of the kitchen of their existence. We need aspiration and great thought-models to lift us.

God has whispered into the ear of all existence, "Look up." There is potential celestial gravitation in every mortal. There is a spiritual hunger in humanity which, if fed and nourished, will lead to the upbuilding and developing of great souls. There is a latent divinity in every son of Adam, which must be aroused before there can be any great progress in individual uplift.

In a factory where mariners' compasses are made before the needles are magnetized, they will lie in any position, but when once touched by the mighty magnet, once electrified by that mysterious power, they ever afterwards point only in one direction. Many a young life lies listless, purposeless, until touched by the Divine magnet, after which, if it nourishes its aspirations, it always points to the north star of its hope and its ideal.

Every faintest aspiration that springs up in our heart is a heavenly seed within us which will grow and develop into rich beauty if only it be fed, encouraged. The better things do not grow either in material or mental soil without care and nourishment. Only weeds, briers, and noxious plants thrive easily.

The aspiration that is not translated into active effort will die, just as any power or function that is not used will atrophy or disappear. The ostrich, naturalists say, once had wonderful wings, but not caring to use them, preferring to walk on the earth rather than mount in the air, it practically lost its wings, their strength passing into its legs. The giraffe probably once had only an ordinary neck, like other animals, but being long used to reach up to gather its food from the branches of trees, it lifted its body in the upward direction until it is now the tallest of all animals, its elongated neck enabling it to gather the leaves from lofty trees.

Something like this takes place continually in human lives. We rise or fall by our ideals, by our pursuit or our disregard of them. The majority of us make bungling work of our living. We spend much precious time and effort catering to the desires of our animal natures and live chiefly along the lines of life's lower aims and opportunities when we might be soaring.

Everywhere we see men making a splendid living, but a very poor life; succeeding in their vocations but failing as men, swerving from their own highest ideals for the sake of making a little more money. On every hand we see people sacrificing the higher to the lower, dwarfing the best thing in them for a superficial material advantage, selling the birthright of the soul's ideal for a mess of pottage.

Is there any reason or intelligence in a man's continuing to turn his ability, his energies, all there is in him, into dollars after he has many times more of these than he can ever use for living and betterment? Is the gift of life so cheap, so meaningless, of so little importance, that we can afford to spend time on things that do not endure,—upon unnecessary material things which so soon pass away,—to the neglect of those that endure? We know that life is our great opportunity to acquit ourselves like men. Yet it is too often into these transient things that we pour the full force of our energies, while we only sigh and "wish" that we could achieve our ideals. We sacrifice much to gain wealth, but practically nothing to realize the outreach of our souls.

Yet the ideal is indeed the "pearl of great price," in the balance with which "all that a man hath" besides is as nothing. The red letter men of the world have always been men of high ideals, to which they were ever loyal: men who have said "this one thing I do," and have put the whole strength of their lives into their effort to realize their ideal.

If from the start you listen to and obey that something within which urges you to find the road that leads up higher; if you listen to and obey the voice which bids you look up and not down, which ever calls you on and up, no matter what its outward seeming, your life can not be a failure. The really successful men and women are those who by the nobility of their example contribute to the uplift, the happiness, the enlargement of life, to the wisdom of the world,—not those who have merely piled up selfish dollars. A rich personality enriches everybody who comes in contact with it. Everybody who touches a noble life feels ennobled thereby.

There is machinery so delicate that it can measure the least expenditure of physical force. If similar machinery could be devised for measuring character many a millionaire would be chagrined at the record of his own just measurement, while many an humble worker would be amazed at the high mark his earnest unceasing efforts to reach his ideal had achieved.

I believe the time will come when not money, but growth, not lands and houses, but mental and moral expansion in larger and nobler living, will be even the popular measure of true riches, real success. The measure of a successful man will be that of his soul; he will be rated in a new sort of Bradstreet, a spiritual Bradstreet, as a large heart, a magnanimous mind, a cultured intellect, instead of as a great check book.

Phillips Brooks said: "The ideal life of full completion haunts us all. We feel the thing we ought to be beating beneath the thing we are. God hides some ideal in every human soul. At some time in his life, each feels a trembling, fearful longing to do some great good thing. Life finds its noblest spring of excellence in its hidden impulse to do one's best."

Every one who substitutes the finer for the cheaper goal, each one who to-day and every day holds to his high ideal despite the stress and turmoil of modern daily living, in such measure hastens the day when such an ideal will be the inspiration of the masses and the power that moves the world.

CHAPTER XIII

HOW TO MAKE THE BRAIN WORK FOR US DURING SLEEP

Would you not think yourself fortunate to have a secretary of great ability and worth absolutely subject, day and night, to your will, and so susceptible to instructions that even your slightest mental suggestion would be faithfully carried out? If you had such a secretary, and knew that in spite of his great ability he would be able to do what you suggested only in proportion to your belief in his power to do so, would you not be careful to entertain no doubts of his ability to carry out your wishes or suggestions?

Now, just substitute for this personal secretary your subconscious self, that part of you which is below the threshold of your consciousness, and try to realize that this self is actually the sort of secretary I have endeavored to describe, capable of carrying out all your desires, of executing all your purposes, of realizing your ambitions, to the exact extent of your belief in its powers, and you will get some idea of what it can accomplish for you.

This secretary is closer to you than your breath, nearer than your heart beat, a faithful servant, walking by your side all through life, to execute your faintest wish, to carry out your desires, to help you to achieve your aims. Every bit of help, of encouragement, of support you give to this other self will add to the magnificence, the splendor of your destiny. On the other hand, all negative, vicious thoughts, all selfishness, greed and envy, all doubts and fears, all the discouraging, destructive thoughts you entertain, will impair and weaken your secretary or servant in exact proportion to their intensity and persistency. In fact it rests with yourself whether your secretary shall be your greatest help, a heavenly friend and assistant, or your greatest hindrance, your worst enemy.

It doesn't matter what we call them,—subconscious and conscious self, or subjective and objective mind, we are all conscious that these are two forces constantly at work in us. One commands and the other obeys. We know that one of these, the subjective mind, does not originate its acts, but gets its instructions from the objective mind, which contains the will power. Experience shows us that the subjective or subconscious mind, which I have called a "personal secretary," is a servant which obeys our will, carries out our wishes, and registers in the brain a faithful record not only of every thought, word and act of ours, but of everything we see, and everything we hear others say.

Coleridge tells of a remarkable instance of the truth of this. A young German servant girl was taken ill with a fever, and in her delirium she recited correctly long passages from famous authors in Latin, Greek and Hebrew. Scholars were called in to hear this uneducated girl speaking fluently tongues of which she had no knowledge in her conscious moments, and to tell if they could what it meant. They were much puzzled and could make nothing of it; but later the miracle was explained. Years before, it seems, the girl had lived in a minister's family, and was accustomed to hear her master recite the classics aloud. She had listened attentively, and her subconscious mind had faithfully recorded every word in her brain, and reproduced what it had heard when the objective mind was quiescent.

Numerous instances might be cited to show that our subconscious mind is the record storehouse of all that has ever happened to us. Every thought, every experience, whatever passes before the eye, or that we see or hear or feel is registered accurately in our brain by our subconscious mind.

Now, if this other self, personal secretary, subconscious mind, or whatever we choose to call it, has such enormous power, why can it not be trained to work for us when we are asleep as well as when we are awake? Have you ever thought of the possibilities of spiritual and mental development during sleep? Has it ever occurred to you that while the processes of repair and upbuilding are proceeding normally in the body, the mind also may be expanding, the soul as well as the body may be growing?

"When corporal and voluntary things are quiescent, the Lord operates," said Swedenborg. The great Swedish philosopher was a firm believer in the activity of the other self during sleep. He claimed that his "spiritual vision" was opened in the unconscious hours of the night.

The Bible teems with illustrations of the activity of the subconscious mind or self during sleep. Warnings are given, work is commanded to be done, visions are seen, plans are outlined, angels are conversed with, courses of conduct advised; and every suggestion made to the soul in the dream state is literally carried out in the waking hours.

Theosophists believe that during sleep the soul or spirit acts independently of the body; that it actually leaves the body and goes out into the night to perform tasks appointed it by the Creator.

As a matter of fact, few people realize what an immense amount of work is carried on automatically in the body under the direction of the subconscious mind. If the entire brain and nervous system were to go to sleep at night all of the bodily functions would stop. The heart would cease to beat, the stomach, the liver, the kidneys and the other glands would no longer act, the various digestive processes would cease to operate, all the physical organs would cease working, and we should stop breathing.

One of the deepest mysteries of Nature's processes is that of putting a part of the brain and nervous system, and most of the mental faculties which were in use during the day, under the sweet ether of sleep while she repairs and rejuvenates every cell and every tissue, but at the same time keeping in the most active condition a great many of the bodily processes and even certain of the mental and creative faculties. These are awake and alert all the time while the sleeper is in a state of unconsciousness.

Most of us probably have had the experience of dropping to sleep at night discouraged because we could not solve some vexing problem to our satisfaction. It may have been one in mathematics during our school days, or, later on, a weightier one in business or professional life, and behold, in the morning, without any conscious effort on our part, the problem was solved; all its intricacies were unraveled, and what had so puzzled us the night before was perfectly clear when we woke up in the morning. Our conscious, objective self did not enter the mysterious laboratory where the miracle was wrought. We do not know how it was wrought. We only know that it was done somehow, without our knowledge, while we slept.

Some of our greatest inventions and discoveries have been worked out by the subconscious mind during sleep. Many an inventor who went to sleep with a puzzled brain, discouraged and disheartened because he could not make the connecting link between his theory and its practical application, awoke in the morning with his problem solved.

Mathematicians and astronomers have had marvelous results worked out while they slept, answers to questions which had puzzled them beyond measure during their waking hours. Writers, poets, painters, musicians, all have received inspiration for their work while the body slumbered.

Many people attempt to explain these things on a purely physical basis. They attribute the apparent phenomenon to the mere fact that the brain has been refreshed and renewed during the night, and that, consequently, we can think better and more clearly in the morning. That is true, so far as it goes, but there is something more, something beyond this. We know that ideas are suggested and problems actually worked out along lines which did not occur to the waking mind. Most of us have had experiences of some kind or another which show that there is some great principle, some intelligent power back of the flesh, but not of it, which is continually active in our lives, helping us to solve our problems.

One of the most interesting instances of this kind is given in the biography of the great scientist, Professor Louis Agassiz, by his widow:

"He [Professor Agassiz]," the writer says, "had been for two weeks striving to decipher the somewhat obscure impression of a fossil fish on the stone slab in which it was preserved. Weary and perplexed, he put his work aside at last, and tried to dismiss it from his mind. Shortly after, he waked one night persuaded that while asleep he had seen his fish with all the missing features perfectly restored. But when he tried to hold and make fast the image it escaped him. Nevertheless, he went early to the Jardin des Plantes, thinking that on looking anew at the impression he should see something which would put him on the track of his vision. In vain— the blurred record was as blank as ever. The next night he saw the fish again, but with no more satisfactory result. When he awoke it disappeared from his memory as before. Hoping that the same experience might be repeated, on the third night he placed a pencil and paper beside his bed before going to sleep.

"Accordingly, towards morning the fish re-appeared in his dream, confusedly at first, but at last with such distinctness that he had no longer any doubt as to its zoölogical characters. Still half dreaming, in perfect darkness, he traced these characters on the sheet of paper at the bedside. In the morning he was surprised to see in his nocturnal sketch features which he thought it impossible the fossil itself should reveal. He hastened to the Jardin des Plantes, and, with his drawing as a guide, succeeded in chiseling away the surface of the stone under which portions of the fish proved to be hidden. When wholly exposed it corresponded with his dream and his drawing, and he succeeded in classifying it with ease."

We are all familiar with examples of the marvelous feats performed by somnambulists. They will get up and dress while fast asleep, lock and unlock doors, go out and walk and ride in the most dangerous places, where they would not attempt to go when awake. Many have been known to walk with sure feet along the extreme edges of roofs of houses, on the banks of rivers, or close to the edge of precipices, where one false step would precipitate them to death.

They will speak, write, act, and move as if entirely conscious of what they are doing. A somnambulist will answer questions put to him while asleep and carry on a conversation rationally.

In this respect the state of the sleep walker is similar to that of a person in a hypnotic trance. He can be acted on from without and remain wholly unconscious. Surgical operations have been performed upon a hypnotized person without the use of anesthetics; and there is no doubt that this also would be possible during profound sleep. The subjective mind is much more susceptible to suggestion when the objective mind is unconscious. There is no resistance on account of prejudice or external influences.

That we are on the eve of marvelous possibilities of treating disease during sleep there is not the slightest doubt. The same is true of habit forming, mind changing, of mind improving, of strengthening deficient faculties, of eradicating peculiarities and idiosyncrasies, of neutralizing injurious hereditary tendencies, of increasing ability. The possibilities of changing the disposition and of mind building during sleep are only beginning to be realized.

The power of the subjective mind over the body is well illustrated by the fact that thoughts aroused in a hypnotized person can very materially shift the circulation of the blood. They can send it at will to any part of the body. The hypnotist can make his subject blush or turn pale, express in his face fierce anger or appealing love. He can at will produce anesthesia in any part of the body so that a needle or knife may be inserted in the flesh without causing the slightest pain. He can so impress the hypnotized person's mind with the belief that the water he drinks is whiskey that he will actually exhibit all the appearance of drunkenness. He can make him believe that the spoonful of water he takes is full of poison so that he will immediately develop the symptoms of poisoning.

The subjective mind is not only capable of carrying out orders but, as has already been shown, every impression made on it is indelible. How often we say, when we cannot recall a well-known name, or the details of some important event or experience, "Well, I cannot think of that now, but it will come to me; I shall think of it later." And how often have the forgotten details flashed into our mind when the occasion had passed and we were thinking of something else. Again and again have we puzzled our brains at night trying to think of some particular thing which had gone out of our memory, only to find it waiting for us in the morning.

We are beginning to realize that all of our experiences during the day, all of our thoughts, emotions and mental attitudes, the multitude of little things which seem to make but a fleeting impression, are not in reality lost. Every day leaves its phonographic records on the brain, and these records are never erased or destroyed. They simply drop into the subconscious mind and are ever on call. They may not come at once in response to our summons, but they are still there and are often, many years after they have dropped into the subconscious mind, reproduced with all their original vividness.

I heard recently of a prominent banker who lost a very important key, the only one to the bank treasures. He claimed that it had not been lost in the ordinary way, but stolen. Suspicion at once attached to the employees. A prominent detective was placed in the bank, and, after watching and questioning every one on the staff, he became convinced that none but the banker himself knew anything about the key.

Every detective is necessarily something of a mind reader, and this one, believing firmly in his own theory, suggested a simple plan for recovering the key. He told the banker to quit suspecting the employees and worrying about burglars getting the bank's treasures, to relax his overwrought mind and go to sleep with the belief that he himself had put the key away somewhere, and that it would be found in the morning. "If you do this," he said, "I believe the mystery will be solved."

The banker, to the best of his ability, did as the detective suggested, and on getting up the following morning he was instinctively led to a certain secret place, and, behold, there was the key. He was not conscious that he had put it there, but after finding it he had a faint recollection of previously going to this place.

The banker's objective or conscious mind was probably busy with something else when he put the key away. Only his subconscious self had any knowledge of what he was doing. Then when he missed the key his fears, his worry, his anxiety, his suspicions and generally wrought-up mentality made it impossible for his subjective mind to reveal the secret to him. But after his mind had become poised and he was again in tune with his subjective intelligence the information was passed along.

Dr. Hack Tuke, a distinguished English authority on the subject. "The memory, freed from distraction as it sometimes is," he says, "is so vivid as to enable the sleeper to recall events which had happened years before and which had been entirely forgotten."

Now, if, as we have seen, the subconscious mind can perform real work, real service for us, why should we not use it especially during sleep? Why should we not avail ourselves of this enormous creative force to strengthen all our powers and possibilities, to piece

131

out, virtually to lengthen our time, our lives? Think what it would mean to us in a life time if we could keep these sleepless creative functions always in superb condition so that they would go on during the night working out our problems, unraveling our difficulties, carrying forward our plans, while we are asleep! We have sufficient proof already to show that they do actual constructive work, but the testimony of Dr. Tuke on this point is of interest. "That the exercise of thought—and this on a high level—is consistent with sleep can hardly be doubted," he writes. "Arguments are employed in debate which are not always illogical. We dreamed one night, subsequent to a lively conversation with a friend on spiritualism, that we instituted a number of test experiments in reference to it. The nature of these tests was retained vividly in the memory after waking. They were by no means wanting in ingenuity, and proved that the mental operations were in good form."

It is now established beyond a doubt that certain parts of the brain continue active during the night when the rest of it is under the anesthetic of sleep. But we have hardly begun to realize what a tremendous ally this sleepless creative part of the brain can be made in our mental development. It is well known that most of the growth of the child, of its skeleton, muscles, nerves and all the twelve different kinds of tissues in its body takes place during sleep, that there is comparatively little during the activities of the day. It is not so well understood that our minds also grow during the night; that they develop along the lines of the ideals, thoughts and emotions with which we feed them before retiring. "All the analogies go to prove that the mind is always awake," says M. Jouffroy. "The mind during sleep is not in a special mood or state, but it goes on and develops itself absolutely as in the waking hours."

As a matter of fact we never awake just the same being as when we went to sleep. We are either better or worse. We changed while we slept. While our senses are wrapped in slumber, the subjective mind is busily at work. It is either building up or tearing down. It is my firm belief that by an intelligent, systematic direction of this sleepless faculty of the brain we can actually make it create for us along the line of our desires. As it is, most people by not putting the mind in proper condition before going to sleep not only do not intelligently use this marvelous creative agency but they destroy all possibility of beneficial results from its action. It is as necessary to prepare the mind for sleep as it is to prepare the body. The following chapter offers some suggestions on this point.

CHAPTER XIV

PREPARING THE MIND FOR SLEEP

Sleep, gentle sleep, how have I frighted thee?

Shakespeare.

Not long ago I heard a young lady say that it was simply impossible for any woman to look charming or to be agreeable right after getting up in the morning. The Rev. Dr. Bushnell declared that "a man must be next to a devil who wakes angry." The way we feel when we awake in the morning depends on how we were feeling or thinking when we went to sleep.

If we retire holding a grudge against a neighbor, with a resolve to "get square" with somebody who has injured us; if we have hatred or jealousy in our heart; if we are envious of another's success, and if we go to sleep nursing these feelings, we awake in a depressed, exhausted state, feeling bitter, pessimistic, irritable, unhappy, about as nearly like a devil as it is possible for a human being to feel. The destroyer was at work all night, running amuck among the delicate brain and nerve cells, furiously tearing down what beneficent Nature had taken such pains to upbuild. But, when we take pleasant, kindly, loving thoughts to bed with us we awake refreshed, in a happy, contented frame of mind. Our sleepless faculties spent the hours in upbuilding, performing friendly offices for us during the night.

Few people ever think of preparing the mind for sleep, yet it is even more necessary than it is to prepare the body. Most of us take great pains to put the latter in order; we undress, take a warm bath, massage the face with some sort of refreshening salve, cold cream, or oil; we make sure that our sleeping room is properly ventilated and that our bed is clean and comfortable, but to the matter of preparing our minds we don't give a thought.

Instead of making our subconscious mental processes build for us in the night, we allow them to tear down much of what we have built during the day. Many of us grow old, haggard and wrinkled in the night, when just the reverse ought to be the case, for Nature herself has ordained that night should be the building, the renewing, time of life.

If we were only to prepare the mind for sleep with the same intelligence and care that we prepare the body; if we were to give it a cleansing mental bath, wiping from memory's slate all black, discordant pictures, all the worries and fears which vexed and perplexed us during the day instead of having the nightmare panorama passing and repassing before us during the night, robbing us of needed rest and neutralizing our upbuilding, recuperative forces, what a difference it would make in our achievement, in our lives!

I know men whose lives have been revolutionized by adopting the practice of putting themselves in a harmonious condition, getting in tune with the Infinite before going to sleep. Formerly they were in the habit of retiring in a bad mood, tired, discouraged over anticipated evils, worrying about all sorts of things. They would discuss their misfortunes at night with their wives and then fall to thinking over the unfortunate conditions in their affairs, their mistakes, and the possible evil consequences that might result from them. Naturally, their minds were in an upset condition when they fell asleep, and, as might have been expected, the melancholy, black, ugly pictures of the misfortunes they feared, vividly exaggerated in the stillness of the night, became etched deeper and deeper on their brains and did their baleful work, making real rest and reinvigoration absolutely impossible. When they reformed their habits, changed their thought, and retired in a peaceful frame of mind with the intention of going to sleep, instead of tossing about thinking of their troubles, their business straightway began to improve. They were stronger, fresher, more vigorous, more resourceful, better able to cope with difficulties, to make plans and to carry them out than when they were depleting their physical and mental resources by robbing themselves of their best friend, Nature's restorative,—sleep.

Many people tell me they cannot stop thinking after they go to bed. Their brains are so active, doing their next day's work, that they cannot stop the mental processes for hours.

Of course you cannot stop all thinking the first night you begin to form the new habit, when you have practiced the old night-thinking habit for years; when perhaps as far back as you can remember you have gone to bed every night worrying, worrying, thinking, thinking, planning, planning ahead for days, for weeks, for months, planning ahead perhaps for the coming year. But if you persist, and make it a cast iron rule to allow no anxieties or fears, no business troubles or discords of any kind to enter your bed chamber, you will succeed in accomplishing your object.

Think of your chamber as the one place sacred to rest, where the things that trouble and harass and vex during the daytime shall find no entrance. Put this legend over the door, or in some conspicuous place where you can see it. "This is my holy of holies, the place of supreme peace and power in my life from which all discord must be shut out." When you undress and lie down, say to yourself, "I have done my best during the day. Now I am going to drop thinking, drop worrying and planning, and get good, refreshing sleep to prepare me for to-morrow's work."

Clear your mind not only of all anxious, worrying business thoughts, but also of all ill will or hatred toward another. Resolve that you will not harbor an unpleasant, bitter or unkind thought of any human being, that you will wipe off the slate of your memory everything you have ever had against any one; that you will forget whatever is unpleasant in the past and start with a clean slate. Just imagine that the words "Harmony," "Peace," "Love," "Good Will to every living creature," are emblazoned in letters of light all over the walls of your room. Repeat them over and over until that other self, that personal secretary just below the threshold of your consciousness, becomes saturated with the ideas they convey, and after a while you will drop into slumber with a serene, poised mind, a mind filled with happy, joyous, creative thoughts.

Of course, until the new habit is fixed, thoughts will intrude themselves in spite of you, but you needn't harbor them. You needn't allow yourself, under any circumstances, to go on thinking about business or any discordant thing after you retire any more than you would allow a madman to slash you with a knife without making any attempt to defend yourself. You can, if you only persist in the new and better way, fall asleep every night like a tired child, and awake in the morning just as refreshed and happy. Your subconscious self will, after a while, carry out your behests without any conscious effort on your part. This sleepless subconscious self is, in fact, one of the most effective agents man has to help him accomplish whatever he desires. Insomnia, for instance, which is the curse of so many Americans, may be entirely overcome by its aid.

If you are a victim of insomnia, and go to bed every night with the thought firmly fixed in your consciousness that you are not going to sleep, you are, to a great extent, the victim of your belief. The conviction in your subconscious mind that there is something the matter with your sleeping ability is largely responsible for the continuance of your trouble.

We know by experience that we can convince ourselves of almost anything by affirming it long enough and often enough. The constant repetition, after a while, establishes the belief in our minds

135

that the thing is true. We can establish the sleep habit just as easily as any other habit.

It is perfectly possible by means of affirmation, the constant repetition in heart to heart talks with yourself to regain your power to sleep normally. Your subconscious self, that side of your nature which presides over the involuntary or automatic functions during sleep, as well as while you are awake, as, for instance, walking, and other things which do not require volition of the mind or especial will power, can be made to obey your commands, or rather suggestions, to overcome insomnia. Say to this inner self: "You know there is no reason why you should not sleep. There is no defect in your physical or mental make-up which keeps you awake. You ought to sleep soundly so many hours every night. There is no reason why you should not, and you are going to do so to-night."

Repeat similar affirmations during the day. Say to yourself, "This sleeplessness is only a bad habit. If you were ill physically or mentally, if you had any serious defect in your nervous system which would give any excuse for insomnia, it would be a different thing, but you haven't anything of the sort. You are simply the slave of a senseless obsession and you are going to break it up. You are going to begin right away. You are going to sleep better to-night, to-morrow night, and the next night. You are going to get through with this bogie you have built up in your imagination which has no existence in reality. Nothing keeps you awake but your conviction, your fear, that you are not going to sleep."

Prepare your mind for sleep in the way already suggested by emptying it of all worry and fear, all envy and uncharitableness, everything that disturbs, irritates, or excites. Crowd these out with thoughts of joy, of good cheer, of things which will help and inspire. Compose yourself with the belief that you will go to sleep easily and naturally; relax every muscle and say to yourself in a quiet drowsy voice, "I am so sleepy, so sleepy, so sleepy." The subconscious self will listen and in a short time will automatically put your suggestion into practice.

It is needless to say that if insomnia is a result of bad or irregular habits, the victim must first of all change his habits before he can expect any relief.

Man is a bundle of habits. We perform most of our life functions with greater or less regularity, so that they become practically automatic. Regularity, system, order are imperative for our health, our success and our happiness. This is especially true in regard to sleep. We must keep regular hours, be systematic in our habits, or our sleep is likely to suffer.

If you play as hard as you work, refresh and rejuvenate yourself by pleasant recreation and a jolly good time when your work is done, and then at a regular hour every night prepare your mind for sleep, just as you would prepare your body, give it a mental bath and clothe it in beautiful thoughts, you will in a short time establish the habit of sound, peaceful, refreshing sleep.

Whatever else you do, or do not, form the habit of making a call on the Great Within of yourself before retiring. Leave there the message of up-lift, of self-betterment and self-enlargement, that which you yearn for and long to realize but do not know just how to attain. Registering this call, this demand for something higher and nobler, in your subconsciousness, putting it right up to yourself, will work like a leaven during the night; and, after a while, all the building forces within you will unite in furthering your aim; in helping you to realize your vision, whatever it may be.

The period of sleep may be made a wonderful period of growth, for the mind as well as for the body. It is a time when you can attract your desires; it is a propitious time to nurse your vision.

Instead of making an enemy of your subconscious self by giving it destructive thoughts to work with, explosives that will destroy much of what you have accomplished during the day, make it your friend by giving it strong, creative, helpful thoughts with which to go on creating, building for you during the night.

There are marvelous possibilities for health and character, success and happiness building, during sleep. Every thought dropped into the subconscious mind before we go to sleep is a seed that will germinate in the night while we are unconscious and ultimately bring forth a harvest of its kind. By impressing upon it our desires, picturing as vividly as possible our ideals, what we wish to become, and what we long to accomplish, we will be surprised to se how quickly that wonderful force in the subjective self will begin to shape the pattern, to copy the model which it is given. In this way we can correct habits which are wounding our self-respect, humiliating us, marring our usefulness and efficiency, perhaps sapping our lives. We can get rid of faults and imperfections; we can strengthen our weak faculties and overcome vicious tendencies which the will power may not be strong enough to correct in the daytime.

If, as now seems clear, the subconscious mind can build or destroy, can make us happy or miserable according to the pattern we give it before going to sleep, if it can solve the problems of the inventor, of the discoverer, of the troubled business man, why do we not use it more? Why do we not avail ourselves of this tremendous

137

mysterious force for life building, character building, success building, happiness building, instead of for life destroying?

One reason is that we are only just beginning to discover that we can control this secondary self or intelligence, which regulates all the functions of the body without the immediate orders of the objective self. We are getting a glimpse of what it is capable of doing by experiments upon hypnotized subjects, when the objective mind, the mind which gets most of its material through the five senses is shut off and the other, the subjective mind, is in control. We are finding that it is comparatively easy while a person is in a hypnotic state to make wonderful changes in disposition, and to correct vicious habits, mental and moral defects, through suggestion.

There is no doubt that so far as the subjective mind is concerned we are in a similar condition when asleep as when in a hypnotic trance, and experiments have shown that marvelous results are possible, especially in the case of children, by talking to them, during their sleep, advising them, counseling them, suggesting things that are for their good.

Parents should teach their children how to prepare their minds for sleep so that the subconscious self would create, produce something beautiful instead of the black, discordant images of fear which so often terrorize little ones before they fall asleep and when they wake up in the dark hours of the night. How often have we noticed the troubled, fear-full expression on the face of a sleeping child, who was sent to bed with anger thoughts, with fear thoughts in its mind after a severe scolding or perhaps a whipping.

A child should never be scolded or frightened, or teased, especially just before bedtime. It should be encouraged to fall asleep in its sweetest, happiest mood, in the spirit of love. Then its sleeping face will reflect the love spirit and the child will awaken in the same spirit, as though it had been talking with angels while it slept.

Children are peculiarly susceptible to the influence of our thoughts, our suggestions to them during sleep. Their character can be molded to a great extent, their ability developed, their faults eradicated, and their weak points strengthened during sleep. In some ways the suggestions made to them in that state have more effect than those made to them when awake, because while the objective mind often scatters and fails to reproduce what is presented to it, the subjective mind gradually absorbs and reflects every suggestion. Many mothers have found this true, especially in correcting bad habits which seemed almost impossible to reach while the children were awake.

If you want to make your child beautiful in character, in

138

disposition, in person, think beautiful thoughts into its mind as it falls asleep; speak to it of beautiful things while it sleeps. I believe the time will come when much of the child's training will be effected during sleep. Its æsthetic faculties, the love of music, of art, of all things noble and beautiful, special talents, and latent possibilities of all kinds will be developed through suggestion.

In the marvelous interior creative forces lies the great secret of life, and blessed is he who findeth it. Doubly blessed is he who findeth it at the start of life.

CHAPTER XV

HOW TO STAY YOUNG

We do not count a man's years until he has nothing else to count.
R. W. Emerson.

The ability to hold mentally the picture of youth in all its glory, vivacity and splendor has a powerful influence in restraining the old age processes.
Old age begins in the heart. When the heart grows cold the skin grows old, and the appearances of age impress themselves on the body. The mind becomes blighted, the ideals blurred, and the juices of life congealed.

Many people look forward to old age as a time when, as a recent writer puts it, you have "a feeling that no one wants you, that all those you have borne and brought up have long passed out onto roads where you cannot follow, that even the thought-life of the world streams by so fast that you lie up in a backwater, feebly, blindly groping for the full of the water, and always pushed gently, hopelessly back."

There is such a thing as an old age of this kind, but not for those who face life in the right way. Such a pathetic, such a tragic ending is not for those who love and are loved, because they keep their hearts open to the joys and sorrows of life; who maintain a sympathetic interest in their fellow-beings and in the progress and uplift of the world; who keep their faculties sharpened by use, and whose minds are constantly reaching out, broadening and growing, in the love and service of humanity. A dismal, useless old age is only for those who have not learned how to live.

Growth in knowledge and wisdom should be the only indication of our added years. Professor Metchnikoff, the greatest authority on age, believes that it is possible to prolong life, with its maximum of vigor and freshness, until the end of its normal cycle, when the individual will gratefully welcome what will be a perfectly happy release. At this point he claims that the instinct of death will supplant the instinct of life, when the bodily mechanism approaches the natural end of normal exhaustion. He believes that men should live and maintain their usefulness for at least one hundred and twenty years.

The author of "Philosophy of Longevity" tells us that man can live to be two hundred years old. Jean Finot says: "Speaking physiologically, the human body possesses peerless solidity. Not one of the machines invented by man could resist for a single year the incessant taxes which we impose upon ours. Yet it continues to perform its functions notwithstanding."

What we have a horror of is the premature death of the faculties, the cutting off of power, opportunity, the decay of the body many years before the close of the life on earth. We shudder at the giving up of a large part of life that has potency of work, of action and of happiness. This horror of senility increases, because life continually grows more interesting. There never was a time when it seemed so precious, so full of possibilities, when there was so much to live for, as in this glorious present. There never was a time when it seemed so hard to be forced out of the life race. We are on the eve of a new and marvelous era, and the whole race is on the tiptoe of expectancy. Never before was the thought of old age as represented by decay and enforced inactivity so repugnant to man.

But why should any one look forward to such a period? It is just this looking forward, the anticipating and dreading the coming of old age, that makes us old, senile, useless.

The creative forces inside of us build on our suggestions, on our thought models, and if we constantly thrust into our consciousness old age thoughts and pictures of decrepitude, of declining faculties, these thoughts and pictures will be reproduced in the body.

A few years ago a young man "died of old age" in a New York hospital. After an autopsy the surgeons said that while the man was in reality only twenty-three years old he was internally eighty! If you have arrived at an age which you accept as a starting point for physical deterioration, your body will sympathize with your conviction. Your walk, your gait, your expression, your general appearance, and even your acts will all fall into line with your mental attitude.

A short time ago I was talking with a remarkable man of sixty about growing old. The thought of the inevitableness of the aging processes appalled him. No matter, he declared, what efforts he might make to avert or postpone the decrepitude of age there would come a period of diminishing returns, and though he might fight against it he would ever after be on the decline of life, going irrevocably toward the sunset, ever nearer and nearer to the time when he should be useless. "The conviction that every moment, every hour, every day takes me so much nearer to that hole in the ground from which no power in Heaven or earth can help us to escape is ever present in my mind," he said. "This progressive, ever-active retrogression is monstrous. This inevitably decrepit old age staring me in the face is robbing me of happiness, paralyzing my efforts and discouraging my ambition."

"But why do you dwell on those things that terrify you?" I asked. "Why do you harbor such old age thoughts? Why are you visualizing decrepitude, the dulling and weakening of your mental faculties? If you have such a horror of the decrepitude, the loss of memory, the failing eyesight, the hesitating step, and the general deterioration which you believe accompany old age, why don't you get away from these terrifying thoughts, put them out of your mind instead of dwelling on them? Don't you know that what you concentrate on, what you fear, the pictures that so terrify you, are creating the very conditions which you would give anything to escape? If you really wish to stay the old age processes you must change your thoughts. Erase everything that has to do with age from your mind. Visualize youthful conditions. Say to yourself, "God is my life. I cannot grow old in spirit, and that is the only old age to fear. As long as my spirit is youthful; as long as the boy in me lives, I cannot age."

The great trouble with those who are getting along in years is that they put themselves outside of the things that would keep them young. Most people after fifty begin to shun children and youth generally. They feel that it is not "becoming to their years" to act as they did when younger, and day by day they gradually fall more and more into old age ways and habits.

We build into our lives the picture patterns which we hold in our minds. This is a mental law. When you have reached the time at which most people show traces of their age you imagine that you must do the same. You begin to think you have probably done your best work, and that your powers must henceforth decline. You imagine your faculties are deteriorating, that they are not quite so sharp as they once were; that you cannot endure quite so much, and that you ought to begin to let up a little; to take less exercise, to do less work, to take life a little easier.

The moment you allow yourself to think your powers are beginning to decline they will do so, and your appearance and bodily conditions will follow your convictions. If you hold the thought that your ambition is sagging, that your faculties are deteriorating, you will be convinced that younger men have the advantage of you, and, voluntarily, at first, you will begin to take a back seat, figuratively speaking, behind the younger men. Once you do this you are doomed to be pushed farther and farther to the rear. You will be taken at your own valuation. Having made a confession of age, acknowledged in thought and act that, in so far as work and productive returns are concerned, you are no longer the equal of young men, they will naturally be preferred before you.

If people who have aged prematurely could only analyze the influences which have robbed them of their birthright of youth they would find that most of them were a false conviction that they must grow old at about such a time, needless worry,—all worry is needless,—silly anxiety, which often comes from vanity, jealousy and the indulgence of such passions as excessive temper, revenge, and all sorts of unhealthy thinking. If they could only eliminate these influences from their lives, they would take a great leap back toward youthfulness. If it were possible to erase all of the scars and wrinkles, all the effects of our aging thoughts, aging emotions, moods and passions, many of us would be so transformed, so rejuvenated that our friends would scarcely know us. The aging thoughts and moods and passions make old men and women of most of us in middle life.

The laws of renewal, of rejuvenation are always operating in us, and will be effective if we do not neutralize them by wrong thinking. The chemical changes caused in the blood and other secretions by worry, fear, the operation of the explosive passions, or by any depressing mental disturbance, will put the aging processes in action.

Whatever we establish as a fixed conviction in our lives we transmit to our children, and this conviction gathers cumulative force all the way down the centuries. Every child in Christian countries is born with the race belief that three score years or three score years and ten is a sort of measure of the limit to human life. This has crystallized into a race belief, and we begin to prepare for the end much in advance of the period fixed. As long as we hold this belief we cannot bar out of our minds the consequent suggestion that when we pass the half century limit our powers begin to decline. The very idea that we have reached our limit of growth, that any hope of further progress must be abandoned, tends to etch the old age picture and conviction deeper and deeper in our minds, and of course the creative processes can only reproduce the pattern given them.

Some men cross the zenith line, from which they believe they must henceforth go down-hill, a quarter of a century or more earlier than others, because we cross this line of demarcation mentally first, cross it when we are convinced that we have passed the maximum of our producing power and have reached the period of diminishing returns.

Many people have what they are pleased to call a premonition that they will not live beyond a certain age, and that becomes a focus toward which the whole life points. They begin to prepare for the end. Their conviction that they are to die at a certain time largely determines the limitation of their years.

Not long since, at a banquet, I met a very intelligent, widely read man who told me that he felt perfectly sure he could not possibly live to be an old man. He cited as a reason for his belief the analogy which runs through all nature, showing that plants, animals and all forms of life which mature early also die early, and because he was practically an adult at fifteen he was convinced that he must die comparatively young. He said he was like a poplar tree in comparison with an oak; the one matured early and died early; the other matured late and was very long-lived.

So thoroughly is this man under the dominion of his belief that he must die early that he is making no fight for longevity. He does not take ordinary care of his health, or necessary precautions in time of danger. "What is the use," he says, "of trying to fight against Nature's laws? I might as well live while I live, and enjoy all I can, and try to make up for an early death."

Multitudes of people start out in youth handicapped by a belief that they have some hereditary taint, a predisposition to some disease that will probably shorten their lives. They go through life with this restricting, limiting thought so deeply embedded in the very marrow of their being that they never even try to develop themselves to their utmost capacity.

Our achievement depends very largely upon the expectancy plan, the life pattern we make for ourselves. If we make our plan to fit only one-half or one-third of the time we ought to live, naturally we will accomplish only a fraction of what we are really capable of doing. I have a friend who from boyhood has been convinced that he would not live much, if any, beyond forty years, because both his parents had died before that age. Consequently he never planned for a long life of steady growth and increasing power, and the result is he has not brought anything like all of his latent possibilities into activity, or accomplished a fourth of what he is really capable.

It is infinitely better to believe that we are going to live much longer than there is any probability we shall than to cut off precious years by setting a fixed date for our death simply because one or both of our parents happened to die about such an age, or because we fear we have inherited some disease, such as cancer, which is likely to develop fatally at about a certain time.

Just think of the pernicious influence upon a child's mind of the constant suggestion that it will probably die very young because its parents or some of its relatives did; that even if it is fortunate enough to survive the diseases and accidents of youth and early maturity, it is not possible to extend its limits of life much, if any, beyond a certain point! Yet we burn this and similar suggestions into the minds of our children until they become a part of their lives. We celebrate birthdays and mark off each recurring anniversary as a red-letter day and fix in our minds the thought that we are a year older. All through our mature life the picture of death is kept in view, the idea that we must expect it and prepare for it at about such a time. The truth is the death suggestion has wrought more havoc and marred more lives than almost anything else in human history. It is responsible for most of the fear, which is the greatest curse of the race.

A noted physician says that if children, instead of hearing so much about death, were trained more in the principles of immortality, they would retain their youth very much longer, and would extend their lives to a much greater length than is now general.

I believe the time will come when the custom of celebrating birthdays, of emphasizing the fact that we are a year older, that we are getting so much nearer the end, will be done away with. Children will not then be reminded so forcibly once in three hundred and sixty-five days that each birthday is a milestone in age. We shall know that the spirit is not affected by years, that its very essence is youth and immortality. In our inmost souls we shall realize that there is a life principle within us that knows neither age nor death. We shall find that old age is largely a question of mental attitude, and that we shall become what we are convinced we must become.

As a matter of fact the average length of life is steadily increasing, because science is teaching men how to live so as to conserve health and youth. Formerly men and women grew old very much earlier than they do now, and they died much younger. We do not think so much about dying as they used to in the early days of this country, when to prepare for the future life seemed to be the chief occupation of our Puritan ancestors. They had very little use for this world and did not try to enjoy life here very much. They were always talking and praying and singing about "the life over there," while making the life here gloomy and forbidding. They forgot that the religion Christ taught was one of joy.

There is no greater foe to the aging processes than joy, hope, good cheer, gladness. These are the incarnation of the youthful spirit. If you would keep young, cultivate this spirit; think youthful thoughts; live much with youth; enter into their lives, into their sports, their plays, their ambitions. Play the youthful part, not half heartedly, but with enthusiasm and zest. You cannot use any ability until you think, until you believe, you can. Your reserve power will stand in the background until your self-faith calls it into action. If you want to stay young you must act as if you felt young.

If you do not wish to grow old, quit thinking and acting as if you were aging. Instead of walking with drooped shoulders and with a slow, dragging gait, straighten up and put elasticity into your steps. Do not walk like an old man whose energies are waning, whose youthful fires are spent. Step with the springiness of a young man full of life, spirit and vigor. The body is not old until the mind gives its consent. Stop thinking of yourself as an old man or an old woman. Cease manifesting symptoms of decrepitude. Remember that the impression you make upon others will react on yourself. If other people get the idea that you are going down hill physically and mentally, you will have all the more to overcome in your effort to change their convictions.

When we are ambitious to obtain a certain thing, and our hearts are set on it, we strive for it, we contact with it mentally and through our thoughts we become vitally related to it. We establish a connection with the coveted object. In other words, we do everything in our power to obtain it; and the mental effort is a real force which tends to match our dream with its realization.

An up-to-date modern woman is a good example of what I mean. She does not act like an old lady, and does not put on an old lady's garb after she has passed the half-century milestone. We do not see the old lady's cap, the old lady's gown of the past any more. Women getting along in years nowadays dress more youthfully and appear younger than their grandmothers did at the same age. They do everything to make themselves appear young. Men are much more likely than women to grow careless in regard to personal appearance as they grow older. They wear their hair longer, they let their beard grow, they stoop their shoulders, drag their feet when they walk, and begin to neglect their dress. They are not as careful in any respect to retain their youthful appearance as women, who re sort to all sorts of expedients to ward off signs of age and to retain their attractiveness.

The habit of growing old must be combated as we combat any other vicious habit, by reversing the processes by which it is formed. Instead of surrendering and giving up to old age convictions and fears, stoutly deny them and affirm the opposite. When the suggestion comes to you that your powers are waning, that you cannot do what you once did, prove its falsity by exercising the faculties which you think are weakening. Giving up is only to surrender to age.

We tend to find what we look for in this world, and if, as we advance in years, we are always looking for signs of old age we will find them. If you are constantly on the alert for symptoms of failing faculties, you will discover plenty of them; and the great danger of this is that we are apt to take our unfortunate moods for permanent symptoms. That is, some day perhaps you cannot think as clearly, you cannot concentrate your mind as well, you do not remember as readily as you did the day before, and you immediately jump to the conclusion that a man of your age must begin to fail, cannot expect as much of himself as when he was younger. In other words, a person whose mind is concentrated upon his aging processes is inclined to draw a wrong conclusion from his temporary moods and feelings, mistaking them for permanent conditions.

The majority of people who are showing the signs of premature aging are suffering from chronic thought poison, that is, the chronic old age poison. From the cradle they have heard old age talk, the reiteration of the old age belief that when a person reached about such an age he would then naturally begin to let up, to prepare for the end. And so instead of fighting off age by holding the eternal youth thought and the vigor thought they have held the thoughts of weakness and declining powers. When they happen to forget something, they say their memory is beginning to go back on them, their sight will soon begin to fail, and they go on anticipating signs of decline and decrepitude until the old age visualization is built into the very structure of their bodies.

Instead of forming the habit of looking for signs of age form the habit of looking for signs of youth. Form the habit of thinking of your body as robust and supple and your brain as strong and active. Never allow yourself to think that you are on the decline, that your faculties are on the wane, that they are not as sharp as they used to be and that you cannot think as well, because your cells are becoming old and hard. He ages who thinks he ages. He keeps young who believes he is young.

We get a good hint of the power of mental influence in the marvelous way in which many of our actresses and grand-opera singers retain their youthfulness, because they feel that it is imperative that they should do so. Had Sara Bernhardt, Adelina Patti, Lily Lehmann, Madame Schumann-Heink, Lillian Russell, and scores of other actresses and singers pursued any other vocation they would undoubtedly have been at least ten, perhaps twenty years older in appearance than they are.

There are too many exceptions to the race belief that man's powers begin to wane at fifty, sixty or seventy to allow oneself to be influenced by it. We really ought to do our best work after fifty. If the brain is kept active, fresh and young, and the brain cells are not ruined by a vicious life, worry, fear, selfishness, or by disease induced by wrong living or thinking, the mind will constantly increase in vigor and power. Men and women whose faculties are sharp and whose minds are keen and vigorous at ninety, and even at a hundred, prove this. I know a number of men in their seventies and eighties who are as sturdy and vigorous physically and mentally to-day as they were twenty years ago. Only recently I was talking with a business man who broke down at forty from over strain but who is now, in his eightieth year, more buoyant and elastic in mind and body than many men at fifty. This man does not believe in growing old because he knows that ten years ago he did not have a bit of the cell material in his body that he has to-day. "Why should I stamp these new body cells with four score years," he says, "when not a single one of them may be a quarter of that age?"

Many of us do not realize the biological fact that Nature herself bestows upon us the power of perpetual renewal. There is not a cell in our bodies that can possibly become very old, because all of them are frequently renewed. Physiologists tell us that the tissue cells of some muscles are renewed every few months. Some authorities estimate that eighty or ninety per cent. of all the cells in the body of a person of ordinary activity are entirely renewed within a couple of years.

One's mental attitude, however, is the most important of all. There is no possible way of keeping young while convinced that one must inevitably manifest the characteristics of old age. The old age thoughts stamp themselves upon the new body cells, so that they very soon look forty, fifty, sixty, or seventy years old. We should hold tenaciously the conviction that none of the cells of the body can be old because they are constantly being renewed, a large part of them every few months. It is impossible for the processes producing senility to get control of the system, or to make very serious changes in the body, unless the mind first gives its consent. Age is not so much a matter of years as of the limpidity, the suppleness of the protoplasm of the cells of the body, and there is nothing which will age the protoplasm like aging thoughts and serenity enemies, such as worry, anxiety, fear, anger, hatred, revenge, or any discordant emotion. If you keep your protoplasm young by holding youthful ideals, there is no reason why you should not live well into the teens of your second century.

Constantly affirm, "I am young because I am perpetually being renewed; my life comes new every instant from the Infinite Source of life. I am new every morning and fresh every evening, because I live, move, and have my being in Him who is the source of all life." Not only affirm this mentally, but also audibly. Make this picture of perpetual rejuvenation and re-creation so vivid that you will feel the thrill of youthful renewal through your entire system.

Some people try to cure the physical ravages made by wrong living and wrong thinking by patching their bodies from the outside. The "beauty parlors" in our great cities are besieged by women who are desperately trying to maintain their youthful appearance, not realizing that the elixir of youth is in one's own mind, not in bottles or boxes. Is there any thing quite so ghastly as to see an old lady (really old because her heart is no longer young), with a painted or enameled face, dressed like a young girl? Such a woman deceives no one but herself. Other people can see the old, dry skin beneath the rouge. They can see the wrinkles which she tries to disguise. She cannot cover up her age with such frivolous pretenses. The painting of cheeks and wearing of girlish frocks do not make a person young. It is largely a question of the age of the mind. If the mind has become hardened, dry, uninteresting, if there is no charm in the personality one is old, no matter what his or her years count.

Idle, selfish women of wealth who live an animal life, who are constantly doing things which hasten the appearance of old age, overeating, over-drinking, over-sleeping, idling life away, having nothing to do but gratify every luxurious whim, are the best customers of beauty doctors, who try to erase the earmarks of old age by "treating" the skin and the hair. Doctoring the effects instead of trying to remove the cause of old age never has been, and never can be, really successful. You cannot repair the ravages of age on the outside. You must remove the cause, which is in the mind, in the heart. When the affections are marbleized, when one ceases to be sympathetic and helpful and interested in life, the ravages of old age will appear in spite of all the beauty doctors in the world.

I know indolent wives of rich men, who cannot understand why they age so rapidly in appearance when living such easy, care-free, worry-free lives. They are puzzled to know why it is when they do not have to work, when they have no cares, when their wants are all supplied without any effort of theirs, they do not retain their youthful appearance many years longer than they do. The fact is those women stagnate, and nothing ages one faster than mental and physical stagnation. Work, useful employment of some sort, is the price of all real growth, of all real human expansion. He, or she, who indulges in continuous idleness pays the price in constant deterioration, physical, mental and moral. A ship lying idle in the wharf will rot and go to destruction much more rapidly than a ship at sea in constant use. Every force in nature seems to combine in corroding, destroying the unused thing, the idle person.

Work, love, kindness, sympathy, helpfulness, unselfish interest—these are the eternal youth essences. These never age, and if you make friends with them they will act like a leaven in your life, enriching your nature, sweetening and ennobling your character, and prolonging your youth even to the century mark.

We are learning that the fabled fountain of youth lies in ourselves; is in our own mentality. Perpetual rejuvenation and renewal are possible through right thinking. We look as old as we think and feel, because thought and feeling maintain or change our appearance in exact accordance with their persistence or their variations. It is impossible to appear youthful and remain young unless we feel young. Youthful thinking should be a life habit.

CHAPTER XVI

OUR ONENESS WITH INFINITE LIFE

He lives best and most who gives God his greatest opportunity in him. If we only knew how to live and move and have our being in Him, to be conscious of this every instant, we should then know what true living means. We should be satisfied, for we should then awake in His likeness.

"Deep within every heart that has not dulled the sense of its inner vision is the belief that we are one with some great unknown, unseen power; and that we are somehow inseparably connected with the Infinite Consciousness."

It is a mental law that thoughts and convictions can only attract their kind. A hatred thought is a hatred magnet and the longer we harbor it, the more steadily we contemplate it, focus our minds upon it, the larger and more powerful the hatred magnet becomes.

In the early days of the great European war a Jewish soldier, in the first line of a Russian battalion, engaged in a man to man fight with an Austrian in the opposing battalion. In their desperate encounter the Russian Jew drove his bayonet through the breast of his opponent. As the latter, an Austrian Jew, fell mortally wounded, with his dying breath he gasped the Hebrew prayer, which begins, "Hear, O Israel." The Russian, realizing that he had killed a brother Jew, overcome with horror, fell fainting on the battlefield. When he regained consciousness he was a raving lunatic.

When will men realize that we are all brothers; that we are all members of the same great human family, children of the same great Father-Mother-God. When will we see that though oceans and continents divide us, though we may speak different tongues, may differ in race, color and creed, yet we are so closely related in thought and motive that our deepest, most vital interests are identical.

Time and again despite all outward differences has that invisible bond of union which binds mankind into one great family manifested itself even on the battlefield. There men who have sabered or shot at and wounded each other have become fast friends and learned to feel their brotherhood. Many and many a time has it happened that soldiers who had been bitter enemies in battle and had tried in every way to kill each other, have found while convalescing side by side that they were really one in sympathy and feeling, brothers at heart and did not know it. If these men had known and seen into one another's soul before the battle as they had afterwards in the hospital they never could have been induced to fire at or to try to injure one another.

In spite of our failures, our blunders, our crimes, the nations are coming closer and closer together. Scientific discoveries, marvelous inventions, the extended use of steam and electricity, the conquest of the air, all these are fast welding the interests of mankind and bringing into close and intimate relation the most distant countries of the globe. The Occident and the Orient are no longer at the ends of the earth. They are beginning to know and to respect each other, and to learn each from the other. They are beginning to realize in its largest sense the truth of Kipling's utterance:

"But there is neither East nor West, Border, nor Breed, nor Birth,
When two strong men stand face to face, tho' they come from the ends of the earth."

Scientists are piling up proof after proof of the unity, not only of mankind, but of every thing in the universe, of the oneness of all life. They are demonstrating that there is but one substance, one eternal force or essence in the universe, and that all we see is but a varying expression of it. Everything about us is merely a modification, a change of form of this universal substance, just as electricity is a manifestation of force in various forms—in its unchained power in rending giant trees and destroying huge buildings, and as harnessed by man in moving trains, in lighting our homes, in furnishing heat for cooking and in many other domestic and industrial devices.

The lesson of lessons for us to learn from this is our inseparable union with the Creator of life, that everlasting, eternal unity of spirit, that oneness with the Father which Christ came to teach.

"I and the Father are one." "I am the vine, ye are the branches." We are as closely united one to the other, and all to the Father as are the branches to the parent stem. When we are conscious of our union, of our co-partnership with the Infinite, we feel an added power, just as the branch feels the force of the life currents flowing into it from the vine. Severed from the parent stem the same branch would not feel so confident. It would soon find that of itself it could do nothing; and in a short time it would wither and die.

152

The moment we pluck a flower from its stem it begins to wilt and fade because it is separated from the source of its life. Cut off from the great chemical laboratory of Nature, from the creative, miracle-working energy of the sun, the soil, and the atmosphere, it dies within a few hours.

The moment we are cut off from our Divine Source we begin to wither, shrivel and die. As long as we remain separate nothing can stop this fatal blighting process. When we are not fed from our Source we are like the branch severed from the parent vine, like the flower plucked from its mother stem.

My experience has shown that people who, from different causes, feel cut off from connection with the Divine Source of things suffer intensely from fear. They are filled with a vague, but overmastering terror which presses upon them with greater force because it is unseen, unknown. They dimly feel that like meteors in the sky which have passed be yond the controlling gravity governing the other heavenly bodies, they are separate, unrelated human atoms without assurance that they are under a protective, guiding, sustaining power.

Victims of extreme nervous diseases are often overwhelmed with a sense of utter isolation, of being cut off from every sustaining force, and they are terror stricken, just as a child who has lost its way, and knows not where to turn. Temporarily, and in a lesser degree, people who are terrified in a thunder storm and rush to a cellar, anywhere to hide themselves from threatened danger, suffer from this feeling of separation, of aloneness.

All who are affected in this way would be greatly benefited by dwelling on such Biblical passages as, "In Him we live and move and have our being," "The Father in me and I in the Father." These are strictly scientific truths. We could not live or move or have any being apart from the Power that made us, that sustains and supports us, and the consciousness of this gives a steadying, buttressing sense of security and safety that nothing else can.

Our individual strength comes from our conscious oneness with Omnipotence, just as our national or corporate strength is derived from union with one another. Each human being is like a drop of water in the ocean. He is not independent. He cannot work alone. Consciously or unconsciously he is a part of the masses all around him. He is touched by other water drops on every side, and his existence, his success is largely dependent upon his union with the others. Even if a drop of the ocean could separate itself from the mass and should try to live its own life in its own way it would soon cease to exist as a drop. A man cannot accomplish much alone. His success depends on his union with other men. His dignity and strength are reënforced by the organization or association of which he is a unit, as a cable is reënforced by the sum of the strength of its separate wires.

"Nature," says Humboldt, "is Unity in diversity of manifestation, one stupendous whole, animated by the breath of life." When we come into conscious realization of the truth that we are a part, the most important part, of the stupendous whole created by God, and that we are working in coöperation with Him, we will come into possession of a power and dignity which will make our lives sublime.

The greatest minds of all ages have drawn their strength from the invisible Source, from their vital connection with the Power which creates, and works through every one of us. They have also believed in the great mission of the race; believed in a divine plan running through the universe which works for righteousness, and shapes the destiny of the race. This faith in the Godward movement of the great human current has characterized even those who did not openly profess any religious faith. Their belief in the divinity of humanity has been a strong factor in their character, and the root source of their power.

This same faith, this unquestioned confidence in the divine cosmic Intelligence, has given more comfort, has brought more peace of mind, and happiness to vast multitudes of human beings than any other thing. Indeed it is the only thing that can bring us true peace, enduring happiness.

There is something beside brain force needed to make a man a real constructive power in the world, and that is his divine connection, his being in the current which runs Godward.

Without this essential, notwithstanding all that the mind and the body can do for us, we feel a void in our being, a great lack, a longing, a yearning for something, we know not what. Without this, even though we have the most complete physical and mental equipment, we are like a new electric car, ready for service, thoroughly equipped in every detail, except the trolley pole, which makes the connection with the electric current. Completion, satisfaction, divine energy can only come from attuning ourselves to something beyond the physical and the mental plane. We must put up our trolley pole and tap the infinite Source of Power or else we are, so far as true progress is concerned, in the position of the car that is not connected with the motor force that alone gives it power to move forward. We must tap the divine current running Godward through contemplation, through prayer, through noble deeds, unselfish service, honest endeavor to live up to our best. We can not make connection with Divine Power through any selfish cause, any greedy deed.

It is a strange thing that human beings will take the chances of cutting themselves off from this mighty current which runs truthward, justiceward, and Godward, and try to make a substitute of their own puny strength.

Yet every time we consciously do wrong, every time we depart from the truth, every time we commit a dishonest, unworthy act, do a mean, contemptible thing, we separate ourselves from this current and lessen the omnipotent grip upon us. We break our connection and become a prey to all sorts of fears and doubts.

Some one has truly said that "when a man has committed an evil act he has attached himself to sorrow." Because of the unity of all life, he has established relationship between himself and the whole human current of vicious influences; he has made connection with all the forces in the universe that conspire to drag him down, to draw him still further away from the Creator and Inspirer of all good.

The converse is equally true. Let a man do a good deed, commit himself to a noble work, and all the creative, uplifting forces will rush to his aid. He will be reënforced by the added power of all others working in the same spirit, on the same plane.

All good things vibrate in unison; they belong to the same family. So all bad things vibrate in unison, and belong to one family. Attract one of them and you attract all the others because they are on the same plane.

A discouraged, despondent mood, for example, makes connection with the whole discouraged and despondent family, the whole failure army, and when we make this connection our entire being is adjusted to the gloomy, discouraged vibration. If we harbor the poverty thought, the fear of coming to want we unite ourselves with all the poverty vibrations in the universe, and whatever has an affinity with poverty rushes toward us through the current we have established.

On the self same principle, let one think cheerful, optimistic thoughts, let him make connections with the current of opulence, of the generous, overflowing abundance supply of the Creator and he allies himself with all the helpful, productive, creative forces in existence.

At one time it was thought that we could get no knowledge or impressions excepting through the five senses, but we know now that there are many other avenues by which we communicate with one another. There is a mental, a spiritual communication which is

155

more intimate, more real than any we can make by physical contact or expression. We can sit beside those who are in sympathy with us for hours without touching them, without a word being spoken, without a look, and yet enjoy the sweetest and most delightful converse. We are conscious that our minds are intercommunicating in a deeper, more subtle, satisfying manner than is possible by means of physical contact or through the senses.

In fact, there are many occasions in life so sacred that we feel mere words would profane, distress, disturb rather than help or comfort. We are aware that they are too coarse to convey the finest sentiments, that they are too bungling, too awkward to carry the expressions of sympathy, of love back and forth from soul to soul that are in tune with each other.

The message of love teaches that the "love of life is a single heart beating through God, and you and me." "One life runs through all creation's veins."

The mind sees beauties which the physical eye never beholds. The mental ear hears harmonies, melodies which the auditory nerve is too gross to perceive. The soul through its closer union with God receives perceptions which even the mind cannot comprehend.

By means of this divine connection through the Great Within of ourselves we can accumulate power that will revolutionize our lives. Right here in our own being we can loose streams of energy infinitely more potent than any physical power.

We know that the great cosmic ether everywhere about us is filled with divine vibrations, charged with spiritual force, and omniscient intelligence which are always waiting to flood our minds when we make the right connections and are ready to receive them.

This cosmic ether or universal substance is the source of all supply, as well as of that divine power, which most people shut out of their lives because they do not know how to unite themselves with it. They resolutely shut their minds to the divine inflow by refusing to believe in anything that is not demonstrable through the senses.

Most of us are very skeptical of the reality of the unseen. We are doubting Thomases, who can be convinced only by the material, by that which we can see or feel.

If children could only be trained in a different atmosphere; if they could be made at the start to reach out mentally into the unseen realities and utilize them for their own purposes, just as we mold and fashion material things, there would be comparatively few failures in life.

It was intended that man should live in perpetual contact with the Power that created him, that would keep him in tune with all

156

that is healthful and good and pure and true, but, unfortunately, we are constantly losing our connection and thus making ourselves impotent, weak, when we might be potent, strong, creative. To live in wireless communication with the divine current that runs through all creation is to be in touch with Divinity indeed, is to be divinely successful.

No power outside of ourselves can cut us off from communication with this current. Even the worst criminals, those who have been cut off from human society may still be one with their Source if they choose. The Creator has not cut them off, has not discarded them. They have broken the connection themselves. The Creator would not blast with a thunderbolt, would not crush with his wrath the most profane wretch that ever lived, even though he should curse Him for creating him. The great love of the Father would still sustain him, keep him alive, feed him, permit the same beautiful sun to shine upon him as upon the greatest saint. All the blessings of nature would still be there for his enjoyment, would be given as freely to him as to the most devoted worshiper.

If we could only grasp this superb truth, our oneness with the great creative principle of the universe it would transform the race. It would banish fear. It would bring peace and harmony into our lives. It would give us a sense of security and satisfaction and happiness such as we never before knew. Until we realize our unity with God and one another we can never grow to our full stature; we can never utilize the manifold powers at our command.

Nor shall we ever reach that glorified man hood which matches the Creator's pattern of the possible man until it is ingrained into every child's nature that he was not only created by his Father-Mother-God, but that he is forever after vitally connected with Him, that He is nearer to him than his own hands and feet, closer than his own heartbeat. This oneness of the child with his Maker is the principle which must ultimately mold the race into perfect beings.

THE END

157